DIVINE DETOURS
WHEN GOD MESSES UP YOUR PLANS

GATEWAY
CREATE
PUBLISHING

DIVINE
DETOURS
WHEN GOD MESSES UP
YOUR PLANS

SION ALFORD

GATEWAY
CREATE
PUBLISHING

DEDICATION

*This book is dedicated to the most influential person in my life.
I have never known someone as humble, as Christlike, nor as loving
as you. You are full of His glory and you are the greatest example of
His bride on this planet. I am honored to be your husband
and best friend. I love you, Shannon Alford.*

Table of Contents

Acknowledgements

Where to start?
Easy.

Gateway Church. I searched for a healthy church when I didn't know what healthy looked like. God and by grace led me to your fields almost a decade ago. You are my Promised Land in so many ways. I am forever grateful. My family is forever grateful.

Thank you, Pastor Robert Morris, for your obedience to "lead and feed" us. The words you share and the leadership you give are building a house that is reaching the world. My life is blessed because of your gift. Thank you.

Pastor Thomas Miller, my friend and oversight. Thanks for believing in the word that God placed in me and helping this book come to life.

John Andersen. Thanks for long hours of editing and thanks for pushing this book through!

Craig Dunnagan. Thanks for your leadership and vision. I am honored to call you friend.

Kathy Krenzien. Thank you for taking care of all the details that brought this project across the finish line.

Blessings to you, George Thomas, for investing in this book. You didn't have to take it on but you did and I am forever grateful.

To the worship staff of Gateway Church. It is an honor to serve along side you, advancing His kingdom. Jason, Kelly, Rita, Dana,

Linda, Josh F., Brandan, Josh C., Courtney, Mary Beth, David M., Alena, Cole, Mark, Ben D., Ben H., Eric, Zach, Levi, Kevin, Rachel M., Rachel R., Janette, Josiah, Walker, Aaron, Jill, Rebecca, Brian, Kristy, Darrell, Katie, Amanda, Ana Paula, Ashley, Coalo, Craig, David S., Erik, Hannah, James, Jeanne, Jenny, Johnny, Loisa, Miguel, Niki, Patrick, Rachel T., Robert, Robyn, Rosemary, Tagi, Tiffany, Tim C., Tim S., Jessica, Natalie, Neeli, Hilary, Amber, Vivian, Martha, and London. You are the greatest worship staff on the planet! I am blessed to serve with you.

Pastor Hayward Miller. Thank you for laying a solid foundation in my life through your teaching and your leadership.

Carlton "Daddy Doc" Schwartz. Thank you for loving and supporting our family. You are a great grandfather to our kids and we are eternally grateful.

Sion Augustus Alford, III, my father. Thanks for being exactly the kind of dad I needed. I love you and thank God for you.

Mom. The first copy of this book is going to you. This book is a result of the prayers you prayed thirty and forty years ago. They are still being answered.

Jeanne Butts. When I was young I didn't pray that I would have a great mother-in-law, but God had mercy on me! The second copy of this book is going to you. You have been a rock for our family through every storm. Thank you for your prayers!

And, lastly, thank you Elizabeth, Si, Mary Catherine, Brooke, Emily, Austin, David, and Caroline. Next to Jesus, you all are the most glorious things in my life. I am blessed to be called your dad.

Introduction
Laying Down Isaac

It's been a long journey. Three days ago, God spoke to me. His voice always dances in my ears like a sweet melody. He said, "Go to the land of Moriah. Take your son Isaac." How I wish He had ended there. However, He didn't.

Isaac. God's promised child. Our hopes hung upon him. Sarah gave birth to him long after women are expected to have children—she was over ninety years old. But God did it. Isaac was our blessing—our miracle.

And now, God wants him back. He wants me to lay down Isaac. He wants me to take his life! God's request is not unusual. All of the other nations around me sacrifice children to their gods every day. But not my God. Yet, He asked.

I thought God gave us this seed, this beautiful young man walking beside me, to be the beginning of a great nation, a great people. I've learned that my God rarely does things the way we expect. His thoughts are always above mine—I'm only a man. And I do trust Him. He has done so many things for Sarah and me. Isaac is reason enough to believe that God is faithful and I can trust Him.

But for three days, I have lived my worst nightmare. It has given me time to ponder. I have wrestled with my faith, but I am going to believe in God's faithfulness—no matter what. I see the sun rise over the mountains to the east of the desert, and I am reminded that God is full of great love and faithfulness.

This time has also given me an opportunity to remember my days in Chaldea. My heart was hungry, starving for something I didn't know even existed. The people around me followed their gods, but they weren't enough. I wanted to worship something greater. Nothing could satisfy me. Emptiness. Longing. Thirsting. Something else had to be out there. Someone different, other . . . holy.

Then I heard His voice for the first time. That voice drives me. Even now, on this awful journey. The voice is loving, gracious, merciful . . . and crazy. That's right—crazy, wild, untamed. It speaks beyond human intellect and wisdom. It is the same voice that told me I would have a child for the first time. Me? I was old, tired, and childless. But that voice told me that I would become a daddy. Craziness. I asked, "Have you run this idea by Sarah?" I later found out that He hadn't. Still He kept telling me I was going to be a father. Then He said I would be the father of a great nation. Now, that's crazy.

Then three days ago, I heard the voice once again—"You know that promise I gave you? The child you wanted for so long and had given up hope of ever having? You know the child I gave you? Now, I want you to give him back—permanently. Forever. No turning back."

If this is a test of faith, I already believed God would give me a child. That was great faith. But now, how can I trust Him when He's told me to sacrifice that same child. Faith? He's asking for everything. If this happens, what will be left to believe in?

I'm sure my servants are confused. I told them, "Stay here with the donkey while the boy and I go over there. We will worship and then come back to you." They look relieved. In fact, they stopped asking questions by the end of our journey's first day. My silence about our purpose and destination probably let them know I didn't want to talk about it. They already think I lost my mind. I certainly can't tell them why we are here or they will know I lost it.

I trust God. But do I have faith? This kind of faith? Until this point, I have based my actions on trust. I trusted God's character, integrity, and person. He has never let me down. He is incapable of it.

Moriah. Of course. How did I miss that one? Of all the places where He could have sent us . . . Of all the mountains in this dusty desert . . . He chose to send us to Mount Moriah! As soon as I saw the mountain, I remembered Moriah means, "God will appear and provide."

Come with me to Mount Moriah. Today God is calling—"Lay Down Your Isaac." Climb the hill, step-by-step with your dreams in tow. At the top we will build an altar, and we will lay down our Isaacs—our visions and promises. Stack the wood. And believe. God is never late, but He is also never early. Wait. God will meet you there, and He will provide.

The Lord directs our steps,
so why try to understand everything along the way?
> —*Proverbs 20:24, NLT*

I've been to "Moriah" many times in my own life.

Even as I write this, I am climbing several Moriahs. I clutch my dreams in my arms, wishing I could scale the heights of Moriah full of faith and trust in God. Instead, I keep searching for a way that is less painful, a path that costs less.

I am not alone. Who wants to see their dreams die? Who gets excited when God asks them to sacrifice their Isaacs?

God gives His most precious gifts; however, then He leads us to an altar and asks us to lay down *everything*, including His own fulfillment of the promises He gave to us. Does this sound crazy? I'm sure it seems counterintuitive, as if it doesn't make sense. But, take it from me, I've had this experience, and I know.

Many years ago, God gave me a dream. In this dream, I saw ministry, music, success, and prosperity. It bore all the usual marks of a divine calling; it was improbable, supernatural, and grandiose. That dream made me feel extraordinary, as if God specially favored

me. With that feeling, I believed that I could take only one path—
I needed to devote myself to making this dream come true.

That's what we're *supposed* to do, isn't it? We should examine
our gifts, discover our calling, pursue our dreams, and never give
up believing. Isn't that right? People tell us that if we do those
things, our dreams will come true.

So I zealously pursued my dream . . . I gave it my all. Through
persistent prayer and diligent devotion, I set out to take hold of
the dream God had promised. I would have my dream, and I'd
trample over anyone or anything that got in the way. I was tena-
cious. I was fervent. I sacrificed. I practiced early and stayed late.

Somewhere along the way; however, the Lord interrupted my
quest for greatness. Like a wrestler, He pinned me to the floor
and let me watch my dream die. When the bleeding stopped and
the dream breathed its last breath, I lay devastated. Broken. Hurt.
Disappointed. Empty.

At the time, of course, I viewed this interruption as anything but
a blessing. It felt like a curse. It was like the feeling we get at the end
of a story, when the hero dies in the last chapter. That's how I felt.
Lousy story.

Here's the good news, though (which I didn't quite understand
at the time): When God is the hero of the story, it never ends in
death. In fact, it is quite the opposite. God's stories always end
in resurrection and life. Jesus' story didn't end at a cross; and
neither does yours. Just as the cross wasn't the end for our Savior,
the death of your dream isn't the end for you. The death of your
dream opens the doorway to something better, more real, and
more life-giving.

Jesus' story didn't end at a cross;
and neither does yours.

And so, my story didn't end with the death of my dream. Eventually, the Lord delivered me from the depths of my own misplaced pursuit and lifted me up to a place of contentment. Ultimately, He resurrected my dream.

Resurrected dreams never look exactly like the original, at least at first glance. Think about Mary Magdalene. Three days after Jesus gave His life, Mary visited the garden grave of her dead "dream." While she mourned, she discovered Jesus' body was missing. At first, she thought thieves had stolen His body. Then Jesus, her resurrected promise, tapped her on the shoulder. "Woman, why are you crying?" He asked. She answered His question with a question: "Are you the gardener?" Her resurrected dream stood directly in front of her and she didn't even recognize Him!

Mary was not alone in her confusion. Think about two men who had spent the last three years closely following the King of the world. They ate meals around hundreds of campfires with Him. They saw Him walk on water. They witnessed as He blessed a few fish and some bread and then multiplied it all to feed thousands of hungry people. And now, three days after they saw their promise killed and sealed inside a grave, a man who had been walking beside them on the road sweeps His hand like a Jedi and opens their eyes to see the resurrected promise. At first, He is unrecognizable, but now He is glowing with resurrected life.

Personally, I don't think of my journey as complete. I know that at some time I may once again have to pick up the pieces of my life. Right now, I am living my dream. By that, I mean that I'm fulfilling God's calling on my life. I'm living out my divine purpose and enjoying what He promised to me many years ago when I was a wide-eyed, idealistic nineteen-year-old sitting in the back row of a little church in Panama City Beach, Florida.

Even so, I haven't "arrived." My journey continues and may take me again through dark valleys and vast deserts. Nevertheless, I am in this spiritual season now and believe that God has given me this opportunity to share what I've learned along the way.

Even as I detail my own experiences, this book isn't about *my dream or me*. Instead, it's about *you* and God's purpose for *your* life. As I tell my story and share the things God has taught me, my goal is to help you live out a better story for your own life.

> Even as I detail my own experiences, this book isn't about *my dream or me*. Instead, it's about *you* and God's purpose for *your* life.

The message of this book is my life's message. It has burned within me for almost two decades. I have studied it, lived it, taught it, preached it, given counsel about it, and sung it. If you haven't yet recognized your dream, or if you're dealing with the discouragement of watching your dreams die, this book is for you. I pray that you will either discover your dream or rediscover God's promises for you, in a way far better than you could have ever imagined. I also pray that this book will change your perspective and your life. I want to point you in the direction of the Dream Giver who will give you strength for your struggles.

1

What Makes Your Baby Jump?

For the creation waits in eager expectation for the children of God to be revealed.
—Romans 8:19, NIV

When God first planted the dream in my mind, it was at a place I never intended to be and at a moment that I didn't expect. I sat on the back pew of a small charismatic church in Panama City Beach, Florida. The church stood only sixty miles from where I grew up, but it was light years away from my small, rural town.

I grew up in Chipley, Florida, which sits in the geographic center of the Florida Panhandle. At sixteen, I became a follower of Jesus in the local Presbyterian Church that my family had attended for generations. No members of my family were in full-time vocational ministry, but they devoted their hearts and treasure to building God's kingdom through that fellowship. Both my dad and grandfather served as elders and deacons. In fact, my great-grandfather helped build the church. Visitors can still find our family's name underneath stained glass windows throughout the building. It was a good church, solid in its theology and in its love for God. In that church, my knowledge of God expanded, and I grew more passionate about serving Him.

Soon after I became a believer, I began to recognize the musical gifts that God had given to me. I had always loved music, but I didn't know then what a major part of my life it would become. My dad was an accomplished musician, who reveled in music of the Big Band Era from the 1930s, '40s and '50s. His mother toured as a classical pianist. So, music was in my blood, in my DNA.

I knew that I loved God and music. What I *didn't* like was the music coming from the three hundred year-old organ in my family's church. It reminded me of a funeral! I liked "real" music—Casey Kasem's "American Top 40" kind of music. I liked Journey, Lionel Richie, Chicago, Kansas, and even a little Sugarhill Gang!

I *knew* there was something deep inside of me—a sound, a song of some sort—I just didn't know how to get it out. The melodies I heard on the radio spoke my musical language, but I struggled with the perversion and the impurity of the lyrics. I wanted to express myself to God and for God with those sounds. I wanted to talk to Him and about Him through music in the language of my time. But I didn't have an example to guide me. Yes, there were pioneers exploring new territory and creating songs that would soon be termed "contemporary Christian music," but I hadn't heard them yet. Remember, I lived in Chipley, Florida!

> I *knew* there was something deep inside of me—a sound, a song of some sort— I just didn't know how to get it out.

One weekend, I visited my older sister in nearby Panama City and went to her church on Sunday evening. It was the first worship service I had ever attended where the congregation sang what people currently call "praise and worship music." Many people had not experienced that style of church music in the mid-1980s. Her church met in a small, storefront building. Once inside, I noticed that they had a live band with an electric piano, bass, drums, and, oh . . . an electric guitar! For a nineteen-year-old music lover, it felt like the Apostle Paul's trip to the third heaven (2 Corinthians 12:2–4). I didn't know if I was in my body or out of my body; all I knew was that I felt like I was in heaven! I'm sure this is how professional athletes feel the first time they play their chosen sport as a child. My heart was on fire. I had tasted my destiny. What I witnessed made my "baby" jump like John the Baptist did before he was born (Luke 1:44)!

What I witnessed made my "baby" jump . . .

Then, in the middle of the music set, the pastor said, "The Spirit of God is here. If you have a request or something you want to say to God, lift up your hands, and talk to Him right now. He is here." When I close my eyes, I can still see the image of all those people, more than a hundred of them, standing with their arms raised toward heaven. This experience was completely new for me. I may have been Presbyterian, but I raised my hands and prayed, "Lord, I just know in my heart that what that guy is doing up there on that piano is what I'm supposed to do. I want to do *that*."

Almost immediately, the worship pastor signaled for the music to stop. He looked across the crowd of people with all of their arms still raised and said, "You there . . . in the red shirt . . . come on down here for a minute."

"Me?" I thought as I looked around for someone else in a red shirt. "Did he just point at me?"

"Yeah, you, the kid looking around."

I did as he told me to do and walked down to the front of the audience. He met me there and began speaking to me one-on-one:

*God heard what you said. His music is in you. You are
going to write songs, and you will play the piano. You're going to
travel all over the world, and God is going to use you to touch the
nations through the songs that you write.*

The things that worship pastor said stunned me. I felt like a dog
that had finally caught a car he was chasing. What am I supposed
to do now? I had asked God for something that had been in my
heart for years—and He had said, "Yes!"

All of these things would make sense if I were already a musician or studying music. But I wasn't! In fact, I was already two years
into a pre-pharmacy degree program. My parents knew that at this
point in my life I was mostly directionless, and they tried not to
pressure me, but music wasn't on any of our vocational plans. Even
more, I hadn't even learned to play an instrument yet. I had taken
a few piano lessons, but that didn't last very long. I could carry a
tune, but my singing voice was less than trained. Even so, when that
worship pastor prayed with me, I left the little church building with
a big promise from God and a dream burning in my bones. God
gave me a fleeting glimpse of the role He wanted me to play in the
world, and I couldn't wait to get started.

When I heard your voice, the baby inside me jumped with joy.
                                        —Luke 1:44, NCV

2
Dream: On!

The greatest achievement was at first and for a time a dream.
The oak sleeps in the acorn, the bird waits in the egg, and in the
highest vision of the soul a waking angel stirs. Dreams are the
seedlings of realities.

—James Allen

In the book of Genesis, we read about Joseph, the patriarch
Jacob's eleventh son. Joseph was only a couple of years younger
than I was when he received his dream. At the age of seventeen, he
experienced a dream or a night vision that he shared with his ten
older brothers (Genesis 37:6–7). Joseph's father gave him the task
of tending sheep, so he likely had this dream while he was in the
fields. Imagine this scene: Joseph sits around a nighttime campfire
with his brothers. As he stares at the coals, he says, "Hey guys!
You're not going to believe this dream I had last night. We were out
in the field binding sheaves of grain and suddenly *my* sheaf rose and
stood upright, while *your* sheaves gathered around mine and bowed
down to it. Pretty cool, huh?"

Obviously, Joseph's older brothers wouldn't be delighted to
hear about his dream. They were already jealous because of their
father's obvious favoritism towards him. But that wasn't all! Joseph
followed up his first dream with a second. Once again, he told his
brothers about his dream, but this time he included his father.

"Listen," he said, "I had another dream, and this time the sun and moon and eleven stars were bowing down to me." (Genesis 37:9, NIV) It didn't take a seer to decipher this dream's meaning—Dad, Mom, the ten older brothers, and one younger brother would be bowing before the great one—Joseph.

What was in Joseph's mind when he decided to reveal his dreams? He clearly underestimated his brothers' anger toward him. What was he *thinking*? If I were to guess, I would say Joseph was trying to turn his God-given dream into a reality. By sharing his promise with everyone, did he prove that he was not yet ready to live out his dream? Clearly, Joseph's dream was bigger than his character could handle at the time.

> Clearly, Joseph's dream was bigger than
> his character could handle at the time.

When I was a small boy, my parents often bought my clothes slightly too big. Over time, it saved them money to buy clothes "with a little growing room." Sure enough, a few months later, my pants and shirts fit perfectly, but they didn't have to buy as many clothes. God usually gives us dreams with a little growing room. Joseph's dream needed a lot of character growth before his dream fit him. Unfortunately, we can't make ourselves grow. Growth is a matter of time and experience, which God supernaturally guides.

Through reading the Bible and through personal experience, I have learned that it is dangerous to try to make your own dreams come true. Instead, we must grow into our calling. We must wait on God. In Genesis 12, God gave Abraham a dream. God said,

> "... go from your country and your kindred and your father's
> house to the land that I will show you. And I will make of you a

*great nation, and I will bless you and make your name great, so
that you will be a blessing. I will bless those who bless you, and him
who dishonors you I will curse, and in you all the families of the
earth shall be blessed"* (Genesis 12:1–3, ESV).

God promised to give Abraham a vast plot of land and a huge
number of descendants who would inherit it. Therefore, Abraham
obeyed God. He left his homeland and traveled to the land of
Canaan, where he lived like a nomad and waited for God to give
him children. After a decade of obedience, Abraham still lived in
a tent and still waited for the sounds of children to fill it. Finally,
Sarah, who had not given birth to any children and who had
grown in years, approached him with what seemed like a reason-
able idea: Maybe God would fulfill the promise through a surro-
gate wife.

*". . . the Lord has prevented me from bearing children. Go in
to my servant; it may be that I shall obtain children by her . . ."*
(Genesis 16:2, ESV).

Abraham took Sarah's suggestion and had intimate relations
with Hagar, who became pregnant. She gave birth to Ishmael, which
means, "God hears."

Ishmael's name is very significant. Abraham and Sarah came up
with their own plan to make God's promise come true, and then
gave God credit for the result! Unfortunately, the result did not
come from God. The birth of the baby caused jealousy and conflict
between the women. It threw Abraham's entire entourage of servants and their families into turmoil. Later, when the chaos became
unbearable for everyone, Abraham expelled Hagar and Ishmael
from the community to fend for themselves.

Throughout history, the descendants of Ishmael have been at
odds with the descendants of Isaac. Even today, the strife continues.

After nearly forty centuries, the world continues to suffer the consequences of Abraham's choice to fulfill God's promise through his own efforts. *The lesson of Abraham and Sarah is simple: when you try to make a dream come true without God, you will birth an "Ishmael."*

> The lesson of Abraham and Sarah is simple: when you try to make a dream come true without God, you will birth an "Ishmael."

Jacob, Abraham's grandson, turned dream-chasing into a lifelong quest! Jacob had a twin brother named Esau. While they were still in the womb, God told their mother that He would give Jacob priority over his brother (Genesis 25:23). Rather than wait for God to fulfill His promise, Jacob schemed to steal the birthright from his older brother (Genesis 25:29–34). To escape his brother's anger, Jacob fled to another country to take refuge with his uncle. Along the way, God gave him a dream or night vision:

> "*. . . I am the Lord, the God of Abraham your father and the God of Isaac. The land on which you lie I will give to you and to your offspring. Your offspring shall be like the dust of the earth, and you shall spread abroad to the west and to the east and to the north and to the south, and in you and your offspring shall all the families of the earth be blessed. Behold, I am with you and will keep you wherever you go, and will bring you back to this land. For I will not leave you until I have done what I have promised you*" (*Genesis 28:13–15, ESV*).

A dramatic experience like this should have given Jacob confidence to wait for God to fulfill His promises, in His own time and in His own way. Instead, Jacob became an expert schemer, prospering in a chess game of trickery with his uncle (Genesis 30:43).

Later in life, Jacob actually wrestled with God in an effort to *take* what God had promised! (Genesis 32:24–32). God injured Jacob to break his will. Only when Jacob could fight no more, only when he could no longer struggle to make his God-given dream come true, did he submit to God's will and way. God freely gave Jacob what he had been striving to take by force his entire life. Strange, isn't it? God had to give Jacob a limp in order to bless him. What is the story of Jacob's lesson for us? *Chasing a dream on your own will eventually leave you wounded. And those wounds may cause you to limp for the rest of your life.*

So Joseph was a true son of his father. Both of them were men with a dream and the unattractive family trait of stubborn self-will. Joseph received a glimpse of his future from God, so he set out to make it come true. First, he declared his dream to his family. However, God doesn't fulfill divine dreams that way. In fact, when we try to fulfill God's promises for Him, the results can be devastating.

3

The Dream Weaver

Father God is neither care-less nor cause-less with how he spends our lives. When he calls a soul simultaneously to greatness and obscurity, the fruit—if we wait for it—can change the world.
—Alicia Britt Chole

Now would be a good time to explain what I mean by a "dream": You often hear the word "dream" used in speeches at awards ceremonies. Oscar winners talk about never giving up on their dreams. Gold medalists talk about chasing their dreams across the finish line. Nearly everyone has dreams that hold the promise of success and happiness. But this is not what I mean by the word. Moreover, I don't think the Bible has this in mind either.

Biographies, business books, and self-help articles contain stories about Oscar winners and Olympians who become successful because they, unlike their peers, use grit and determination to turn their childhood fantasies into reality. These stories promise that we, too, can become successful if only we are willing to sacrifice everything for the sake of our dreams. We receive the message that self-determination, personal responsibility, and ambition will deliver us the results we want. However, that message is far from biblical. The message of the Bible is *far more exciting*. According to God's Word, a "dream" is not a wish we make for ourselves; it is God's revelation of the purpose for our being!

We read in the Bible that God knows each person intimately. Millions have lived and died since the beginning of time, and today nearly seven billion people walk the earth. It might be hard to imagine that God knows you personally and intimately, but the Bible says He knows more about you than you know about yourself:

> *O Lord, you have examined my heart*
> *and know everything about me.*
> *You know when I sit down or stand up.*
> *You know my thoughts even when I'm far away.*
> *You see me when I travel*
> *and when I rest at home.*
> *You know everything I do.*
> *You know what I am going to say*
> *even before I say it, Lord (Psalm 139:1–4, NLT).*

In fact, no detail about you is too small or too insignificant for God (Matthew 10:30). Even more, you can never measure how much God values you. How do humans usually measure the value of something? If it's rare, it is worth more. Gold has more value than concrete because gold is more difficult to obtain—it is rare. And you are rare, uncommon, and maybe even a little unusual. You are one of a kind. No one exactly like you has ever existed. You are precious and *valuable*! How valuable? When it came time to purchase you, God gave His only Son!

As an individual, you are of great worth to God.

For some people, that concept is hard to understand. Even more, God, your Creator, not only loves you and made you in His image, *He likes you!* God takes delight in you as a unique individual. You are important to Him, and God grieves when you do not connect with Him. God also designed you with a special purpose in mind. King David put this amazing thought into a song:

> *For you formed my inward parts;*
> *   you knitted me together in my mother's womb.*
> *I praise you, for I am fearfully and wonderfully made.*
> *Wonderful are your works;*
> *   my soul knows it very well.*
> *My frame was not hidden from you,*
> *when I was being made in secret,*
> *   intricately woven in the depths of the earth.*
> *Your eyes saw my unformed substance;*
> *in your book were written, every one of them,*
> *   the days that were formed for me,*
> *   when as yet there was none of them (Psalm 139:13–16, ESV).*

David chose the same Hebrew words and phrases to describe how God "forms" and "weaves," as artisans did when they created beautiful pottery or tapestries. With his song, David celebrates God's creation—you. God wove His design for your life into the spirals of your DNA. He has a major part for you to play in His plan for the world. Nevertheless, you have an even bigger place in God's plan than your physical or mental abilities. He gave you many talents and skills before you were born, but *God continues to work in life.* He is still creating and forming you into the person He wants you to be.

> *May God himself, the God of peace, sanctify you through and through. May your whole spirit, soul and body be kept blameless at the coming of our Lord Jesus Christ. The one who calls you is faithful, and he will do it (1 Thessalonians 5:23–24, NIV).*

He will do it. God will finish His work in you. God created you, formed you, and designed you to complete His purpose for you. You can succeed if you allow Him to remove all of the unnecessary things from your life.

Michelangelo once said of one of his sculptures, "I saw the angel in the marble and carved until I set him free." In the same way, God will carve until He has set the *real* you free to fulfill His calling and purpose on your life.

> *And I am certain that God, who began the good work within you, will continue his work until it is finally finished on the day when Christ Jesus returns (Philippians 1:6, NLT).*

I have been calling this special purpose a "dream." This "dream" is nothing less than seeing yourself in the future doing what God created you to do. God reveals that dream to inspire and empower us to think differently from the world. God pulls back the veil of mediocrity to give us a glimpse of our greater destiny.

This "dream" is nothing less than seeing yourself in the future, doing what God created you to do.

While your dream is supernatural because it comes from God, He doesn't hide it from you as though it is a mystery. In fact, many people think about dreams that way. They expect a beam of light from the skies, the rumbling voice of God, or rolling mists from heaven. But God usually shows us our dream through many smaller promises. I like to call these "micro-dreams." I don't mean that they're insignificant or unimportant; instead, I think these dreams are more common and frequent. We can have several of them at the same time. A dream may be a promise from God that you will prosper in your finances one day. Salvation for a friend or loved one may come as a message from God. Maybe God will tell you about a future spouse. Whatever the dream, big or small, the principle remains the same—*God has plans for us.*

When the Babylonians took the Jews into exile, the Jews fell into despair. Far away from the Land of Promise God had given to Abraham, the people of Israel wondered if He had given up on them. But God reassured the people of his unconditional love through Jeremiah the prophet

> *"For I know the plans I have for you,"* says the LORD. *"They are plans for good and not for disaster, to give you a future and a hope"* (*Jeremiah* 29:11, NLT).

"Plans" in this verse are plural. God has many plans for you; some big and lofty, and others small and commonplace. Either way, God wants you to know His plans and dreams for you.

At some point in life, God whispers a dream in every person's ear. Sometimes He tells people early in life, sometimes later, and always at a time when we are ready to hear. God spoke to Abraham when he was over seventy years old. Joseph heard God at seventeen. God called a teenage David from among his flocks to anoint him the shepherd of Israel. He called young Samuel with a voice in the night. God commissioned Moses from a flaming bush when he was over eighty years old.

Most people do not experience God's call in a dramatic way like these people from the Bible. Dreams come in many different ways. Others in the Bible, and many today, would describe their dreams as an awakening—as though God gently blew on a spark that then grew into a flame. These dreams had always been there inside of them. *Only* those believers who remained connected with God . . . and *only* as He orchestrated their lives . . .

and *only* at the right time did they become aware of His purpose for their lives.

For me, that happened in the back row of a little church in Florida. At that moment, God's dream resonated in my spirit and became *my* dream. Your experience will be different—a unique event and a dream made just for you.

God's dream may have already sprung up within you. On the other hand, you might still be waiting. Either way, I encourage you to keep two undeniable facts about God-given dreams in mind. First, God has a purpose for you that will show itself as a dream—eventually. Second, *you're not in charge of creating that dream, discovering that dream, or fulfilling that dream. Only God is.*

> You're not in charge of creating that dream, discovering that dream, or fulfilling that dream. Only God is.

Delight yourself in the Lord, and he will give you the desires of your heart (Psalm 37:4, ESV).

Your job is to delight in the Lord. Then follow as He leads you. This verse does not tell you to delight yourself in the Lord, and then He will give you anything you desire. Instead, the Psalmist says that God will *give* you *desires*. Desires that your heart can run with. He will give you dreams and a passion for His purpose. Our job is to delight and take joy in *Him*, not the dream.

4

Dream Detours

There are two kinds of people: those who say to God, "Thy will be done," and those to whom God says, "All right, then, have it your way."
—C. S. Lewis

A divine dream can be a little intoxicating. Many Bible heroes felt a sudden rush of awareness and excitement when they received a dream. And they all responded in similar ways: they tried to *do* the promise God had given them, and they set out to fulfill their dreams themselves.

In my case, I think God's supernatural intervention kept me from going to such extremes. I thought about stopping the path toward becoming a pharmacist to enroll in a Bible college, or maybe even a music school. I submitted the application to pharmacy school, but my heart really wasn't in it. I wanted to get moving toward the dream God had given me. I thought, "What could five more years of pharmacy school possibly teach me about being a musician, worship leader, and psalmist?"

So I started learning how to play the keyboard. In addition, I joined the youth worship team at my church. I sold some of my prized possessions—my ATV and all of my hunting gear—and I purchased keyboards and sound equipment. I wanted to learn, so I soaked up music knowledge like a sponge. While I studied hard, I also took music lessons and volunteered at church. I tried to become a worship leader and songwriter. I went from not knowing how to play an instrument to becoming the worship leader of a large church youth group.

Then, before I knew it, I had completed my two-year, pre-pharmacy degree and the pharmacy school accepted me as a student. Now I faced a dilemma—what should I do next?

My choice should have been clear—at least according to the advice I was reading in some Christian self-help books. I had very little interest in pharmacy, and my exciting experiences with worship ministry didn't give me any more desire for a medical profession. I loved music and serving the Lord through worship more. I knew I had the drive and ability to pursue a ministry in worship music.

Then something happened. I had a dream—an actual, fall-asleep-and-wake-up-sweating kind of experience. It wasn't a supernatural vision in the middle of the night. Nevertheless, I believe God was guiding it. I dreamed that alligators surrounded me. All night long, as I tossed and turned, alligators chased me up trees, into cars, and into the safety of my house. When I finally awoke in the morning, I felt strongly that I should follow through with my application to the pharmacy program at the University of Florida, whose mascot is an alligator!

So I obeyed God instead of pursuing my own personal desires. It made very little sense to me at the time, but I was determined to do this God's way. And on *His* timetable. I committed to five more years of pharmacy school. Yes, I could have used that time to follow the "normal" career path of a worship pastor: Bible school, music school, and then seminary. However, God set me on a different path. Pharmacy school was *His will*, which incidentally, looked nothing like *His promise*. Many times the will of God doesn't look like the dream He gives or the promise He has made to us.

Many times the will of God doesn't look like the dream He gives or the promise He has made to us.

Admittedly, sometimes I strayed from the path. That's usually when life knocked me down.

When I first arrived at the University of Florida, I approached the pastor of a nearby church and asked if I could serve in their worship ministry. He assigned me to the sound team, which felt like a punch in the stomach. Instead of standing up front, singing, playing my instrument, and leading others to the throne of Christ in worship, I was coiling wires and lugging amps late at night. Instead of leading a band, I was twisting knobs at the *back* of the room. That challenged who I thought I was, because I had confused my gifts and calling with my identity. I felt myself slipping even further away from my dream.

Soon, however, I found peace in working behind the scenes. I had found the good place in life in the center of God's will. I was serving where God wanted me *at the time*, which gave me contentment despite feeling far removed from what I first wanted to do. Before long, I said to myself, "I'm going to do everything I can to make this church's worship leader sound good and look good." I bought a book on sound reinforcement and started reading about parametric equalization, frequencies, and resonance, and how to mix a live performance. I took delight in bringing musical knowledge to the technical world, and I began to see the twenty-four-channel mixer as more than a tool. *That soundboard became my musical instrument.*

Over time, I would move on to another phase of my schooling—both in pharmacy and in life—and I would quickly forget those lessons. I had to learn them all over again in another context, but eventually I began to understand what God was doing. Pharmacy school wasn't an accidental detour, it was a *divine detour*! God made it a necessary part of my path. Those extra five years of schooling didn't deter me from my dream, they prepared me for it. Something was happening inside of me. Something invisible. Something greater than the dream itself. God was working within me to transform me. He was preparing me for the promise because, apparently, I wasn't ready for the promise! I still had some growing to do before I could live out my dream.

Remember the definition I gave of "dream" earlier? It is nothing less than seeing yourself in the future doing what God created you to do.

When you see your dream, what do you see? Yourself! However, you don't see yourself as you are right now. You see something different and more inspiring than your present. That is what makes it a "dream" and not "*déjà vu*."

So how can a dream come true? Something has to change, and that "something" is you. If you don't seem to be going in the direction of your dream, realize that God is taking you through situations and circumstance—character detours—divine detours—that will work to change you.

> So how can a dream come to true? Something has to change, and that "something" is you.

The bigger the dream, the more we have to change in order for it to become a reality. In the dream, we look different. In dreams, we see ourselves accomplishing something that we are not accomplishing today. Moreover, we are fulfilling a need that we are not fulfilling today. A dream is you in the future doing something bigger, better, and different. The greater the calling, the more detours we may have to take in order to arrive at the promise. Why? Because *more change* is needed. What we think is a detour, God sees as an opportunity to shape and mold us into the person He wants us to be.

> What we think is a detour, God sees as an opportunity to shape and mold us into the person He wants us to be.

When we face these alternate routes, we often feel as if we missed God or that we are not in His will. In fact, we are right in the middle of His perfect will. Your present circumstances, no matter how frustrating or painful, stand as proof that you have some changing to do.

5

Bitter or Better?

Freedom from pain is not the only indicator of whether or not something is beneficial.

—*Ravi Zacharias*

I always did well in math and not so well in English. One thing I learned in basic geometry is this: The shortest distance between two points is a straight line. To get from point A to point B in the shortest amount of time, travel in a straight line. No detours. No pit stops. No bathroom breaks. Get there, and get there now.

Here's some bad news—God's math and our math are not always the same. The shortest distance between two points may be a straight line, but it's not necessarily the *best* line. For example, the path God had planned for Joseph was anything but an easy ride to the top. Nevertheless, it was exactly what Joseph *needed*.

Soon after Joseph shared his dream with his family, his brothers conspired to kill him.

They said to one another, "Here comes this dreamer. Come now, let us kill him and throw him into one of the pits. Then we will say that a fierce animal has devoured him, and we will see what will become of his dreams" (Genesis 37:19–20, ESV).

Thankfully, Joseph's oldest brother talked them out of killing him. Instead, the brothers sold him as a slave to a passing caravan of Ishmael's descendants. A few days later, Joseph found himself on the auction block in Egypt, very different from standing over his bowing siblings. Detour? Will of God? Promise? Dream?

You have to admire Joseph. He didn't lose heart. A high-ranking government official named Potiphar purchased Joseph to work in his household. Instead of trying to escape and return home, Joseph took on his duties with poise, faithfully serving his owner. God blessed his work, and Potiphar quickly took notice of Joseph's intellect, eventually promoting him to house-hold manager. Joseph discovered his place—in the center of God's will.

> ... the Lord blessed the Egyptian's house for Joseph's sake; the blessing of the LORD was on all that he had, in house and field (Genesis 39:5, ESV).

We can learn something here—pits are often doorways to palaces. They are God-designed detours. They are divine detours. While we don't always see them that way, we must recognize that what may look like a dark, damp dungeon might really be a divine disguise. God designs those detours to reveal something. He is showing us who we really are. It is at the bottom of a pit, at God's detour, that we find out what we are really made of.

> Pits are often doorways to palaces.
> They are God-designed detours.

In Joseph's case, his pit revealed his true character. He was a leader waiting for the right time. Joseph was an administrator in need of something to administrate. He was talent waiting for a platform on which to perform.

As the chief administrator of Potiphar's personal affairs, Joseph occupied one of the most powerful positions in all of Egypt. He might have thought this position would be the way that God would fulfill His promise. Masters often freed a favored slave upon their death, and even gave them a sizeable portion of the estate as a reward for faithful service. Joseph's dream was so close he could almost reach out and touch it. But then Joseph suffered a cruel irony. He was expecting a straight road and suddenly hit a sharp curve. He couldn't steer and correct his vehicle fast enough.

Potiphar's wife tried to seduce Joseph, And Joseph refused to betray the trust of the man who had treated him so well. Even more, Joseph said he didn't want to sin against God:

> *". . . How then could I do this great evil and sin against God . . . ?" (Genesis 39:9, Amplified).*

Nevertheless, to cover her sin and take revenge for Joseph's rejection, Potiphar's wife accused Joseph of trying to rape her! So Potiphar sided with his wife and had Joseph put in prison, where he languished for the next few years.

Detour? Will of God? Promise? Dream?

These circumstances must have been devastating for Joseph. He had done nothing to harm his brothers, yet they sold him into slavery. Then the slave traders hauled him off to a foreign country. He had been guilty of no crime in Egypt. In fact, he had been above reproach, even looking out for the interests of the man who kept him as a slave. Yet there he lay in a prison, paying a severe penalty for his honesty, integrity, and loyalty. The world must have felt like a very cruel place.

At this point in the journey, Joseph must have had some serious concerns about how wonderful it was to serve God.

"Well, God, so this is what I get for serving You? If this is what You allow to happen to those who love You, I sure would hate to be Your enemy! Thanks a lot for the dream, God. I have had nothing but bad happen since you *blessed* me with such a wonderful dream! I think it might be easier to go back to being a sinner. Being a saint is not what it was hyped up to be."

These thoughts come to us too easily at some point in our journey with God. Detours make us think that way sometimes. Remember, we get to see Joseph's story from beginning to end. But Joseph *lived* that story. He didn't know that a happy conclusion was coming. In fact, just when he thought the dream was closer to fulfillment, life knocked him down *again*! Even more, he probably felt as if he was pushed *even further* from its fulfillment. *Another painful detour.*

Becoming a leader of prisoners is *probably not* the "success" most people aspire to achieve. In many ways, Joseph's dream looked very dead when he found himself stripped of his rank, fitted with chains, thrown into prison, forgotten by everyone, and forsaken by justice. From all outward appearances, Joseph's journey had ended in failure, and his dream was nothing more than a teenage delusion.

> *But the Lord was with Joseph and showed him steadfast love and gave him favor in the sight of the keeper of the prison (Genesis 39:21, ESV).*

Nevertheless, Joseph was not alone in that prison. For the first time, we can see the results of an established, healthy relationship between Joseph and God. God's reward for Joseph's faithfulness in the face of persecution and suffering was this—*God's presence and God's favor.*

Somewhere on the floor of that prison, a chained, rejected, and bruised Joseph realized that what looked like failure was not final. His destiny did not rest in the hands of his superiors or his leaders.

It rested in the hands of a faithful God. A God who is near. A God who is close. Joseph rose from the ashes of his pain and continued to believe—*not in the dream, but in the Dream Giver.*

And the keeper of the prison put Joseph in charge of all the prisoners who were in the prison. Whatever was done there, he was the one who did it. The keeper of the prison paid no attention to anything that was in Joseph's charge, because the Lord *was with him. And whatever he did, the* Lord *made it succeed* (Genesis 39:22–23, ESV).

So then, those who suffer according to God's will should commit themselves to their faithful Creator and continue to do good (1 Peter 4:19, NIV).

> Doing the right thing and walking in God's will can be costly. It will cost you something, sometimes everything.

Sometimes doing the will of God leads to suffering. Sometimes it leads to persecution. Sometimes it leads to crucifixion. Does that sound encouraging? I am sure it doesn't, but it is true. Doing the right thing and walking in God's will can be costly. It will cost you something, sometimes everything.

"You can enter God's Kingdom only through the narrow gate. The highway to hell is broad, and its gate is wide for the many who choose that way. But the gateway to life is very narrow and the road is difficult, and only a few ever find it" (Matthew 7:13–14, NLT).

Why do only a few find the gate that leads to God's kingdom? Why do only a few walk on the pathway of His will?

Because, as Joseph did, they find the path is often narrow and difficult.

You may be able to relate to Joseph's rejection and disappointments. I know I can. I once heard, "No one can achieve greatness until they have felt the bitter hand of betrayal and disappointment."

Joseph felt this. David felt this. Moses and all of the prophets felt it. Even the King of Kings, Jesus, felt it. It is not a question of whether you will ever feel betrayed or disappointed, but how will you handle it?

It is not a question of whether you
will ever feel betrayed or disappointed,
but how will you handle it?

Have you found yourself at the bottom of a pit in certain areas of your life? Whether someone threw you in there or you fell in through some other way, know this—the pit has a purpose. Take inventory of your life. Ask God to show you the character of your heart. What is He revealing to you? Look closely. You can find answers. Somewhere in the mess, God has a message. Somewhere in the pain, He has a plan. And it likely has something to do with His calling on your life.

Will you lie on the prison floor of rejection and become bitter, or will you allow the divine detours of life to make you better?

It's your choice.

6

Ambition or Burden?

We are not called to pursue our dreams. We are called to pursue the Dream Giver.

When we awaken to the purpose that God has chosen for our life, when God's dream first forms in our mind, our first response is to grab hold of it with a double-fisted, white-knuckle grip. At that point, we attach our identity to the dream so that we can barely distinguish between the dream and ourselves. And when something or someone threatens the dream, *we feel threatened.* When something derails the dream, we feel sidelined by God. If the dream should die, we mourn its passing just as deeply as though we were standing at our own graveside.

It was through the death of my own dream that I came to understand a great theological truth: *God never told anyone to pursue a dream. Instead, He invites us to pursue Him.*

God never told anyone to pursue a dream.

His desire is that we pursue *Him.*

He calls us to pursue a relationship with *Him.*

God never gives dreams to substitute for Himself.

We cannot gain our significance from what God has given us *to do.* We don't find fulfillment or joy in the dream, we find fulfillment and joy *only in Him.*

Even so, it's tempting to latch onto the dream—with all the greatest, most godly intentions. Then we quickly forget that God gave us the dream. We often cling to the gift for life and forget that life can only come from the Giver of Gifts. When that happens, the Lord must pry us loose from the dream to remind us that He is our supply and He alone is our inheritance.

O Lord, You are the portion of my inheritance and my cup;
You maintain my lot.
The lines have fallen to me in pleasant places;
Yes, I have a good inheritance (Psalm 16:5–6, NKJV).

God will separate us from our dream in one of two ways: either we can surrender the dream to God, or we can let our own ambition squeeze the life out of the dream until it dies in our arms. Either way, the Lord will not allow something else to replace Him, even if it's the dream He originally gave to us.

> The Lord will not allow something
> else to replace Him . . . even if it's
> the dream He originally gave to us.

Abraham had great ambition. After more than a decade of waiting and with a wife who was well beyond the age to bear children, he tried to fulfill God's promise and fathered Ishmael. The trouble with replacement children is that you can't kill them or ignore them. Consequences live on, and you may have to deal with them forever.

Jacob had great ambition. He cheated his brother and then spent the next couple of decades scheming. The more he clutched his dream, the more chaotic and futile his life became. He lived most of his earlier years feeling cheated and paranoid, no matter how much he prospered.

Moses had great ambition. He thought that he would become the deliverer of the Hebrews by killing an abusive Egyptian slave driver. Rather than lead the Israelites out of bondage, he was exiled to the far side of the Arabian Desert for forty years (Exodus 2:11–14). Moses had been educated to rule a nation. However, there among the sheep, he found himself supremely qualified to do *nothing*.

Joseph had great ambition. David had great ambition. Paul had great ambition. Timothy had great ambition. To each of these men, God gave a priceless gift. He allowed their ambitions to lead them to a place where their dreams died on seemingly endless, lifeless detours.

For these men, it was the only way. When their dreams died, they surrendered to God. They mourned what felt like their own deaths. In addition, they learned, some more quickly than others, to draw their strength, their joy, their fulfillment, and their identity from God alone. When they learned to pursue God rather than their dreams, they learned the great lessons of God's kingdom:

> . . . *man does not live by bread alone; but man lives by every* word *that proceeds from the mouth of the Lord (Deuteronomy 8:3, NKJV; cf. Matthew 4:4,).*
> *But seek first the kingdom of God and his righteousness, and all these things shall be added to you (Matthew 6:33, NKJV).*

We can learn a valuable lesson here: God has not called us to carry ambitions; He has called us to carry burdens (Ross, 2016).

The pit is where God turned the ambitious heart of Joseph-the-Dreamer into the burdened heart of Joseph-the-Redeemer. An ambition is different from a burden. Ambitions motivate us from the outside—we want to accomplish because *we* want the glory. Burdens motivate us from the inside—we want to accomplish because it brings *God* glory.

Ambition seeks a position without a process. Ambition wants the prize without the pain. Eventually ambition will deny the will of God and seeks its own way.

> Ambitions motivate us from the outside—we want to accomplish because *we* want the glory. Burdens motivate us from the inside—we want to accomplish because it brings *God* glory.

Is all ambition bad? I am not sure. As I study the Scriptures, I can't find any good news surrounding ambition. The only reference I can find that even resembles something positive is this:

> *. . . and to make it your ambition to lead a quiet life: You should mind your own business and work with your hands, just as we told you . . .* (1 Thessalonians 4:11, NIV).

That doesn't sound like the ambition I usually encounter. Any ambition that I have personally experienced looks the opposite of a quiet life, minding one's own business, and working as under authority. My ambitions have always led me to hectic, unrestful circumstances, striving to climb the ladder of success, and doing what is best for me—and me only.

Usually, when the Bible mentions ambition, it describes the kind that I have experienced. Ironically, we usually think of the word in English, preceded by another word—selfish. The authors of the Bible had an awareness of that kind of ambition as well:

But if you harbor bitter envy and selfish ambition in your hearts, do not boast about it or deny the truth. Such "wisdom" does not come down from heaven but is earthly, unspiritual, demonic. For where you have envy and selfish ambition, there you find disorder and every evil practice (James 3:14–16, NIV).

Here's a powerful truth: Wherever there is envy and selfish ambition, disorder and every evil practice will result. Why disorder? Because God has created order and it involves surrender, not self-promotion. People who practice selfish ambition sit on the throne of their own lives—kings and queens of nothing. However, a real throne does exist. Moreover, God designed it for God alone. Our dreams easily become idols that we worship. Moreover, their altars are littered with the ashes of broken marriages, families, and churches.

On the other hand, *selfless* ambition creates success and salvation for others at the expense of *self*. The Bible calls selfless ambitions *burdens*.

Burdens are simply selfish ambitions that have died and been resurrected as selfless. These ambitions have been through the fires of God's timing. Burdens are ambitions that have experienced divine detours that often pose as pits and prisons. That's where burdens are born. Ambition is the marble hiding the masterpiece. The Master must chip and hammer it until it disappears, revealing the true burden.

Burdens are ambitions that have
experienced God-designed detours
that often pose as pits and prisons.

People with burdens are unstoppable because their motivations are pure and their actions always radiate the fruit of the Spirit. No burnout happens when carrying godly burdens. There is no anxiety or worry. The burden is His, and it is light.

> *"Take my yoke upon you and learn from me, for I am gentle and humble in heart, and you will find rest for your souls. For my yoke is easy and my burden is light"* (Matthew 11:29–30, NIV).

As soon as Moses, David, Paul, Joseph, and Abraham realized the foolishness and selfishness of their ambitions, they reached a place of rest and peace. They got their priorities straight, and their dreams received resurrection power. Their dreams became godly burdens fueled by a desire to please God rather than their own ambitious desires. That's what God does to sacrificed dreams and promises. He resurrects them and transforms them into burdens guided by the yolk of His voice.

The dreams and promises of Abraham, Jacob, Moses, and Joseph came to life bigger and more powerful than ever. Even more, these men no longer felt the need to nurture or protect their dreams. They became secure in God's provision so that the dreams became afterthoughts as they pursued God. Never again did they doubt God would fulfill His promise, even in the face of impossible circumstances and million-mile detours.

7

A Gift Catalog

If you want to know the purpose of a thing, never ask the thing.
—*Myles Monroe*

I love Christmas. More accurately, I love getting gifts. I really do. After I finished reading Gary Chapman's book, *The Five Love Languages*, getting gifts was clearly one of my top love languages. If you want to show me that you love me, give me a gift!

One of my favorite Christmas memories happened when my dad would hold a wrapped present up to his forehead and try to guess what was in the package. He could do it almost every time! He would pick up the wrapped gift, shake it, smell it, and put his ear to it. Then he would tell us what was inside without ever opening it. That's an amazing feat for a kid to see!

However, that's not what we are supposed to do with the gifts God has given to us. We need to open them. Unwrap them. Imagine that I handed you a gift, brightly wrapped with a great big bow on the top. You might shake it, listening for telltale thumps or rattles. On the other hand, you might carefully test its weight. If I told you to open it, you might tear right into it with wild abandon, or you might be a paper-saver, gently loosening the tape and slowly unfolding each crease. Alternatively, you might be a great guesser like my dad.

Whatever way you unwrap gifts, I doubt you would set the gift aside or put it away in a closet. Yet, this is what many of us have done. We didn't do it with last year's Christmas gifts, of course. We did it with something worth much more. We have set aside or ignored our spiritual gifts—the supernatural abilities God specifically chose to give each of us.

Don't doubt that you have a gift. Maybe you were born with it. Maybe you've practiced, honed, and developed it. Maybe you received it through prayer or laying-on of hands. Whatever the case may be, you have one. And often, whether it's due to lack of interest or awareness, or simply because you don't understand what God has given you—these gifts remain wrapped, still in the box.

Years ago, God laid on my heart a desire to help people not only unwrap their gifts, but also understand the purpose behind them. A great responsibility comes with these divine abilities. This is incredibly important, especially for those who have not yet discovered their dream, because a gift will provide a clue for you. It's a sign that points you directly toward your dream. That's because spiritual gifts and divine dreams work together. God fulfills your dream when you are operating in your gifts. If you can discover, recognize, and understand your gifts, you will have a better understanding of your purpose.

<blockquote>
God fulfills your dream when
you are operating in your gifts.
</blockquote>

Scripture speaks strongly about understanding our gifts. Paul says:

Now concerning spiritual gifts, brethren, I do not want you to be ignorant: (1 Corinthians 12:1, NKJV).

Paul always had a unique way of saying things, but I'm from the southern part of the United States, where we might say something like, "Don't be stupid about your gifts." Take a good look at them. What do they say about you? What can they tell you about God's dream for you? Before you can answer either of those questions, you simply need to unwrap your gifts—before you can decide the *purpose* of your gifts you need to know what they are.

Before you start tearing off the paper, step back for a moment, and look at spiritual gifts as a whole. It's easier and wiser to examine yourself after you've examined what Scripture has to say about you, so let's go there first. Consider two types of gifts. I will call them *charisma* gifts and *doma* gifts. The name for the first group likely sounds familiar to you, but let me elaborate. In the Greek, these gifts are called a *charisma*, which comes from the base word *charis* meaning "grace." Sometimes people refer to them as "grace gifts." These are the types of gifts with which we are most familiar.

This is important, so don't miss it: Just like salvation, God gives these charisma gifts by grace, based on nothing but God's goodness. *Strong's Concordance* defines them simply as "a spiritual endowment, a religious qualification, or a miraculous faculty." I like that—a miraculous faculty. Your gift is a miraculous faculty given by God, through no merit of your own. *And here's what a gift does—it helps you do what a normal person can do—only better, supernaturally better.*

> ## And here's what a gift does—it helps you do what a normal person can do— only better, supernaturally better.

For example, think about singing. Anyone with functioning vocal chords can sing, but if we're honest, we'll admit that not everyone *should* sing (at least not publicly!). Some people *can* sing, and often *do sing*, but they don't have the gift of singing. On the other hand, someone with the gift of singing possesses a supernatural quality that mere talent cannot explain. This is a *charisma* gift.

Examples of this kind of gift appear frequently in the New Testament. Paul said to the Corinthians:

> *To each is given the manifestation of the Spirit for the common good. For to one is given through the Spirit the utterance of wisdom, and to another the utterance of knowledge according to the same Spirit, to another faith by the same Spirit, to another gifts of healing by the one Spirit, to another the working of miracles, to another prophecy, to another the ability to distinguish between spirits, to another various kinds of tongues, to another the interpretation of tongues. All these are empowered by one and the same Spirit, who apportions to each one individually as he wills* (1 Corinthians 12:7–11, ESV).

Paul names nine gifts: wisdom, knowledge, faith, healing, miracles, prophecy, distinguishing of spirits, tongues, and interpretation of tongues. In his letter to the Romans, he gives another list. Romans 12:6–8 mentions prophecy, service, teaching, encouragement, giving, leadership, and showing mercy. The variety of gifts found in these two lists leads me to believe that neither is all-inclusive—there may be more. Just because the Bible doesn't mention a gift doesn't mean you should discount it. In fact, if we expand our search to the Old Testament we find the following:

> *Then Moses said to the people of Israel, "See, the LORD has called by name Bezalel the son of Uri, son of Hur, of the tribe of Judah; and he has filled him with the Spirit of God,*

with skill, with intelligence, with knowledge, and with all craftsmanship, to devise artistic designs, to work in gold and silver and bronze, in cutting stones for setting, and in carving wood, for work in every skilled craft. And he has inspired him to teach, both him and Oholiab the son of Ahisamach of the tribe of Dan. He has filled them with skill to do every sort of work done by an engraver or by a designer or by an embroiderer in blue and purple and scarlet yarns and fine twined linen, or by a weaver—by any sort of workman or skilled designer . . ." (Exodus 35:30–35, ESV).

These artisans were given gifts of not only wisdom and knowledge, but also craftsmanship. In his chapter on the subject of spiritual gifts, one author wrote:

> If God supplied supernatural gifts for every skill needed in the building of the Tabernacle and its furnishings, will He not also supply in this age a spiritual enablement to correspond with every kind of service needed in building the Holy Temple of which Christ is the Foundation and Chief Cornerstone? Might this not include the composing of spiritual music, the mastery of musical instruments that aid worship, the writing of Christian literature that edifies spiritually, and even the building of structures that serve for worship and teaching? (Duffield and Van Cleave, 1983, 356).

If Paul took the time to list all possible gifts, he might still be writing! Even so, those are all what I call *charisma* gifts. They are skills, supernatural abilities, and we all have at least one.

I also want to explore a second type of gift: the *doma* gift. This word sounds much less familiar to English speakers than *charismata*, but it also comes from the Greek. *Doma* also means gift, but whereas *charismata* indicates, "grace gifts," *doma* specifies a more general term meaning "that which is given." Here, you'll see this word in action:

> So Christ himself gave the apostles, the prophets, the evangelists, the pastors and teachers, to equip his people for works of service, so that the body of Christ may be built up (Ephesians 4:11–12, NIV).

A significant distinction exists in this passage from the *charisma* gift. The *doma* gift seems to stress the *character* of the gift rather than the quality of the gift. In fact, the word translated "gave" in the passage above is sometimes also translated as "allow" or "appoint." This use of the word demonstrates that *doma* gifts are *appointed. They are positional. And they bring with them authority.* Charisma gifts bring neither position nor authority, and this is a key observation, because on this point the kingdom of God and the church differ from the systems of the world.

The world accepts that if you're the best singer, you lead the choir. If you can hit the notes, then you'd better take over leadership. If you are the best athlete, you should be the captain of the team. If you have the most persuasive personality, you should be the boss. However, in the kingdom of God, Jesus gives *doma* gifts and appoints people for leadership. Even more, your appointment has more to do with your character rather than your ability. It's based on who you *are*, not what you can *do*. Your charisma does not guarantee a position for you in the kingdom, nor does it give you authority.

Think about it this way—God promotes character, not talent.

God promotes character, not talent.

Sure, talent is important, but it's not the most important factor God considers when He promotes or appoints someone. The Lord looks at the heart of a person (1 Samuel 16:7). He looks past an individual's abilities and credentials to examine character.

One reason many organizations, including churches, businesses, and governments, do not succeed is because human nature tends to appoint talent and gifting over strength and genuineness of character.

Does that mean we should promote people who do not have talent or gifting? Certainly not, but it should not be the *reason* for promotion. I know many people God has blessed with charisma gifts who are operating in a *doma* gift. To be a pastor of a church or to lead an organization, a person must have certain charisma gifts, but they must submit those gifts to God's appointment for there to be proper order.

Much of the chaos and disorder seen in many organizations, including churches, stems from promoting talent and gifting without accurately discerning character. The result is an organization built on personality and charisma instead of character and Christlikeness.

> Much of the chaos and disorder seen in many organizations, including churches, stems from promoting talent and gifting without accurately discerning character.

Why do organizations promote people like this? Why do churches in particular do it? The answer is simple—it brings *instant* results. When God was ready to anoint a new king over Israel to replace the rebellious Saul, He sent the prophet Samuel to the house of Jesse in Bethlehem to anoint a new king. As seven of the sons of Jesse paraded before the prophet, Samuel saw how tall and strong all the sons appeared.

"Surely this one must be the one," he must have thought. "He is tall, dark, and handsome."

"No," the Lord whispered.

"Well, this one must be the one. Look how he leads; he is a Type A personality and very confident in his leadership."

"No," the Lord whispered. "Not this one."

"Well, surely the Lord's anointing is on this one," as Samuel looked on Eliab.

"No. Not him."

"Oh wow, then this one must be the one. His name is Shammah! The name Shammah means 'astonishment,' so this has got to be the one!"

Samuel, you are missing it. I don't look on the appearance or on the height of a man's stature when I get ready to appoint and anoint someone to a place of honor. I do not see what man sees. Man looks on the outward appearance. Man looks at the 'wow' factor and the talent. But I look at what can't be seen. I look into the hidden parts of a man's heart and see the character of the person. You know them for what they do. I know them for who they are (1 Samuel 16:7, paraphrased).

This imagined conversation illustrates perfectly that God promotes character, not talent and gifting. The kingdom of God operates like this. We can see this pattern throughout Scripture in the lives of Joshua, Gideon, Moses, Paul, Timothy, and many others. Moreover, when we see this principle violated, the outcome is never good.

Properly understanding your gifts can help you discern what your dream is. It can give you a glimpse of the purpose for which God has designed you. However, those gifts are not the sum total of who you are. Remember, you are *not* your gift!

8

The Anointing

If you want to live in the fullness of God's anointing, fill your mouth with the word of God.

—Joyce Meyer

Why do we call some gifts "spiritual" when it appears that people outside the church also have them? How are these gifts any different from natural-born talents? Many reality show contestants are extremely talented singers. We've all seen great athletes accomplish amazing feats. You may know someone incredibly gifted in business. Everything that person touches seems to turn to gold. We clearly recognize gifted people.

A difference exists, however, between having a *gift* and God *anointing* someone. Let me clarify what I mean by "anointed." To do this, we'll have to do some theological digging, and examine some Greek terms used in the New Testament. Look at this important passage of Scripture, in which Jesus says,

"*The Spirit of the Lord is upon me,*
  because he has anointed me
  to proclaim good news to the poor.
He has sent me to proclaim liberty to the captives
  and recovering of sight to the blind,
  to set at liberty those who are oppressed" (Luke 4:18, ESV).

Jesus said this about Himself, quoting from the book of Isaiah. If we look at the word translated as "anointed," we discover the Greek word *chriō*, which is the word Greek writers used for sacramental or religious anointing. In fact, "Christ," the title comes from *chriō*, which means, "anointed one." *Strong's Concordance* defines *chriō* as to "smear or rub with oil." You probably think of the word "anoint" as a very religious term; however, for the common person of Jesus' time, the word simply meant to "smear or rub with oil."

Though the *Louw-Nida Greek-English Lexicon* has some differences from *Strong's*, it says the word involves "supernatural sanctions, blessing and endowment—to anoint, to assign, to appoint, assignment, appointment" (Louw and Nida, 1996, 1:483). Clearly, the word is not simply a holy word, but it does have divine meaning as it relates to the calling of those whom God endowed with gifts. I may upset a few people here, but from this study, it is clear to me that the anointing *is not* the Holy Spirit.

The anointing *is not* the Holy Spirit.

If you came from a religious background similar to mine, you probably learned this about anointing. I have heard it said many times, and many times, I have said it, "The anointing is here," when referring to the Holy Spirit. To be more accurate, we should simply say, "The Holy Spirit is here."

The anointing is nothing more than "a rub or a smear" of the Holy Spirit. It is a mark of His divine working. Jesus said, "The Holy Spirit is upon me, *because* he has anointed me . . ." (Luke 4:18). We might also say it like this: "The Holy Spirit is upon me, because he has marked me for a divine flow, a specific assignment, or a particular appointment."

The anointing "marks" us for a divine flow of God's Holy Spirit. I like to think of it as a target for the Holy Spirit. It acts as a magnet for the divine, inspired supernatural flow of God's Spirit. The anointing is something that the Holy Spirit is attracted to when released by God to manifest His nature and character into the natural realm in which we live.

There is a lot packed into that sentence. Read it again: The anointing is something that the Holy Spirit is attracted to when released by God to manifest His nature and character into the natural realm in which we live.

> The anointing is something that the Holy Spirit is attracted to when released by God to manifest His nature and character into the natural realm in which we live.

When the Holy Spirit "marks" us, He sets us apart and appoints us or assigns us to a specific task. God does the anointing *with* the Holy Spirit. Jesus says, "The Spirit of the Lord is upon Me, because He [the Lord] anointed Me." God anointed Jesus to do specific things:

> *"The Spirit of the Lord is on me,*
>   *because he has anointed me*
>   *to proclaim good news to the poor.*
> *He has sent me to proclaim freedom for the prisoners*
>   *and recovery of sight for the blind,*
> *to set the oppressed free,*
>   *to proclaim the year of the Lord's favor"* (Luke 4:18–19, NIV).

You may think I am stretching the meaning when it comes to applying this idea to our lives. That passage of Scripture clearly refers to Jesus, *the* anointed one! But I want you to remember this:

As redeemed people, we are one with Christ, and the Holy Spirit has also anointed us.

> *Now it is God who makes both us and you stand firm in Christ. He anointed us (2 Corinthians 1:21, NIV).*

In addition, remember:

> *As for you, the anointing you received from him remains in you, and you do not need anyone to teach you. But as his anointing teaches you about all things and as that anointing is real, not counterfeit—just as it has taught you, remain in him (1 John 2:27, NIV).*

If you are in Christ, then He has anointed you for a specific task. He has set you apart, "rubbed and marked" you, for a particular calling. This anointing will "teach" you about all the things related to your calling.

> He has set you apart, "rubbed and marked" you, for a particular calling. This anointing will "teach" you about all the things related to your calling.

As I think back on the early years of God's calling on my life, I knew that God called me to music and ministry. I found myself particularly attracted to the ministry of several worship leaders and church leaders at the time. I studied them. I studied how they sang, how they wrote music, and how they preached and taught. I observed them from a distance through their books, music, videos, and recordings. I even had the opportunity to serve in several of their ministries. Moreover, I learned first-hand about the anointing that was on their lives.

The anointing taught me.

Nevertheless, did I want their anointing? No. It was theirs. I knew God had anointed me for something, but I didn't know exactly what it was at the time. What I did know was that when they operated according to the anointing God put on *their* gifts, I learned something about the gifts and callings of God in *my* life. The anointing that I had received from the Lord taught me *through them*.

I think it is important to say this here: Do not lust or desire after the anointing that is on someone else. That is dangerous and those desires, if not fully submitted to God, will mislead you. Then you will find yourself wanting what they have without being willing to pay the price to receive it.

> Do not lust or desire after the
> anointing that is on someone else.

Often, people look at the platform or see the performance of an anointed person and they want what that person has. However, those people do not have that same anointing to be able to operate from that particular place of influence. There is nothing wrong with having a desire to do similar things that we see others doing for the kingdom of God. However, those desires become toxic when they lead us to lust after someone else's anointing.

I remember a conversation I had with a young worship leader several years ago. That zealous young man said, "Pastor Sion, I am here to serve you. I want what you have. The anointing that is on your life is also on mine, and I am here to receive a double portion of the anointing as I serve you in the same way Elisha served Elijah!" I explained to this eager believer that there was much still to be learned. First, I was no Elijah. Moreover, he was certainly no Elisha. Second, the anointing I received was for me, not for him.

He had his own anointing from God, and mine was not about to be "transferred" to anyone.

However, I realize what the young man was communicating. He wanted to learn and receive from me. I encouraged him over the years to learn from those who had a similar anointing, but not to lust after or desire someone else's anointing or position. He learned well and is fulfilling his unique calling today in a tremendous way.

9

Anointed Gift

When God creates men and women, He designs them to fulfill their function and gives them certain qualities and characteristics that enable them to perform His intended purpose. These abilities are yours before birth.

—Myles Monroe

The Holy Spirit sets us apart and anoints us for a specific purpose, but we must ask ourselves this simple question: "What does He anoint?" He anoints the gifts within us! He "marks, smears, or rubs" our gifts, consecrating them for a divine flow of the supernatural power of God.

Again, there is a difference between having a gift and having an *anointed* gift. Gifts can entertain people; anointed gifts *inner-change* people.

> Gifts can entertain people;
> anointed gifts *inner-change* people.

This anointing, this mark, and this touch of the Holy Spirit transforms a gift into a powerful tool—a miraculous faculty. Why does God anoint a gift and make it supernatural? To answer that, we must return to the issue of *purpose*. You might not know your purpose right now, but God gave you specific gifts to equip you to fulfill a critical role in His kingdom—whatever it might be. Not only do your gifts equip you to *accomplish* your purpose, they also help you to *discover* your purpose.

These gifts are like the tools a master builder uses when constructing a house. Maybe this is why I love tools and hardware stores. I love walking down the aisles, smelling the construction dust. It brings me back to my roots. Where I grew up, every man was a handyman. I grew up surrounded by men who could fix anything—sometimes even if it wasn't broken! My mom's father was a master handyman, a man of many tools. He could fix anything, and his workshop was full of tools. I loved it there!

After he died, our family received the task of cleaning out his enormous tool shed. What I remember the most about that adventure was discovering all of his tools. Since many of them were not labeled "router" or "drill press," we had to figure out what each tool was by its design. As we examined each tool, we could figure out its purpose.

We should examine our spiritual gifts (our tools) to determine their purpose. Just as my family looked at the aspects of a tool to discover its use, examining our gifts can help us discern what God designed us to do. I can't declare your purpose or tell you how to use your spiritual tools. Only God knows those things. Nevertheless, in God's Word, you can find direction. You will see that all people have some common purposes.

I learned something else about tools as a young man: You can use tools for things outside of their intended design. Even if you can do the job using the wrong tools, the result is often not excellent. In addition, the process is not as efficient. Often, the wrong tool leads to making worse the problem that you were originally trying to fix. You can complete almost any project, if you have the right tools. Let God position you in the right place at the right time so that He can use your gifts (tools) to the greatest effect.

Paul understood this important truth. He was a "spiritual" tool man. He wrote his letter to the Church in Corinth to help each person get in the right place at the right time, so that each person's gifts (tools) could be used in the correct way.

> *I wish that all of you were as I am. But each of you has your own gift from God; one has this gift, another has that (1 Corinthians 7:7, NIV).*

Paul shares something else important:

> *. . . Each person is given something to do that shows who God is: Everyone gets in on it, everyone benefits. All kinds of things are handed out by the Spirit, and to all kinds of people! . . . (1 Corinthians 12:4–11, The Message).*

God did not give us our gifts so that we could entertain ourselves, put on a show, or gain fame. He gave them to us so that we might *show the world who He is!*

> *Each of you should use whatever gift you have received to serve others, as faithful stewards of God's grace in its various forms (1 Peter 4:10, NIV).*

The gift God has given you has a purpose attached to it. The gift He has given you has souls attached to it. Your gift is all about people—*other* people! Your gift is about advancing the kingdom of God, not the kingdom of *self*.

Your gift is all about people—*other* people! Your gift is about advancing the kingdom of God, not the kingdom of *self*.

In Ephesians, Paul lists those *doma* gifts mentioned earlier and then follows up with the reason for those gifts:

> *. . . for the equipping of the saints for the work of service, to the building up of the body of Christ (Ephesians 4:12, NASB).*

Paul goes a step further:

> *. . . until we all attain to the unity of the faith, and of the knowledge of the Son of God, to a mature man, to the measure of the stature which belongs to the fullness of Christ (Ephesians 4:13, NASB, emphasis added).*

This sentence may be difficult to understand, but it points towards the idea that our individual gifts build God's kingdom. All of us contribute toward one great, all-encompassing purpose: *to see Jesus manifested and revealed in our world!* The world needs to see Christ's Body, the Church, grow to the same stature as Jesus in all of His fullness! Isn't that what the Body of Christ is supposed to be—the earthly representation of Jesus to the world? Yes, it is.

Our gifts reveal Jesus. God designed our gifts to show the world *who He is*. Because God designed our gifts specifically and uniquely, they fit our unique calling. The manifestation of Jesus through each of us is unique and genuine. Only I can reveal Him the way He designed me to reveal Him. Only you can reveal Him the way He designed you to reveal Him.

Only I can reveal Him the way He designed me to reveal Him. Only you can reveal Him the way He designed you to reveal Him.

For the creation waits in eager expectation for the children of God to be revealed (Romans 8:19, NIV).

There is an empty spot in each person that only God can fill when He reveals Himself. So, exactly *how* is He revealed? It happens when we, the children of God, *manifest* Him. He has placed gifts and tools in each of us that are designed to reveal Jesus. *The real Jesus.* Creation is waiting in eager expectation for that revelation.

I can relate to Paul's passion to see the Body of Christ awakened to the reality of this mysterious revelation he wrote about:

I have become its servant by the commission God gave me to present to you the word of God in its fullness—the mystery that has been kept hidden for ages and generations, but is now disclosed to the Lord's people. To them God has chosen to make known among the Gentiles the glorious riches of this mystery, which is Christ in you, the hope of glory (Colossians 1:25–27, NIV).

There is a hope in you.
The mystery is alive.
It is Christ in you.
Reveal Him.

10

The Great Divide

The glory of God is humanity fully alive.

—*Irenaeus*

Since we understand that we have something inside of us that needs to be revealed to the world, how do we do that? How do we show this "mystery" to people around us? Before we explore those questions, a personal story might help to understand this divide between the natural and supernatural realms.

During the last year of pharmacy school, we were required to work at several medical institutions around the state of Florida. This internship required us to change locations every two months. Sometimes we would have to move and live in cities several hundred miles away from our homes. At one such location where the school assigned me to spend two months during the summer, I had a difficult time renting an apartment. No one wanted to offer a two-month lease. The medical institution was not in a large, populated area, so an extended-stay hotel wasn't an option either.

The only place I could find that would rent a room for such a short period was through a real estate agency. They had a house rented to a family, and it had an attached "mother-in-law" suite, which included a bedroom, a small kitchen, and a bathroom.

Perfect. A single, large door connected the suite to the main house. Both sides could lock.

I signed the contract, moved my belongings in, and set up to stay there. It was ideal . . . until about 3:00 a.m. the first night. I woke up in a pool of sweat. I immediately searched for the thermostat. However, there was only one thermostat in the house . . . and it was on the other side of the locked door!

I soon realized that the husband and wife on the other side of that door weren't very happy to have a college student living on the other side of their living room wall. They were a little upset with the realtor for renting it. So they decided to take it out on me by turning off the A/C when they weren't home—which turned out to be about ninety percent of the time! Let me tell you, those were a *long* two months!

That wall was a barrier to what I desired—the thermostat. It was "a great divide." I couldn't control the atmosphere in my environment without getting into the atmosphere of the room next door, which enclosed the thermostat.

In much the same way, our spiritual universe contains two rooms, as it were, or two realms: the natural realm, where we physically live and move every day, and the spiritual realm. These two realms exist at the same time, and each contains the things that specifically belong there. All the things belonging to the spiritual realm exist on one side of the dividing wall. These are things like God, angels, love, joy, provision, salvation, healing, wisdom, and knowledge. Our side of the wall belongs to the natural realm, where you and I are limited to our five senses. We can see, hear, smell, taste, and touch. Nevertheless, whatever we do, we can't get through the wall to the spiritual realm on our own.

God has to communicate that He is there and show us who He is. For God to share Himself and teach us about things in the spiritual realm, there must be a doorway, a portal, or a conduit—a way to manifest the things of the spiritual realm in the realm of our senses.

So how does God do it?

He shows Himself through nature, through the order of life, through the Bible, or through Jesus. But God also created us in His image (Genesis 1:27, Ephesians 4:24, Colossians 3:10), so we are capable of being conduits to the supernatural. Even after the fall of humanity, which distorted much of God's image in us, we still reveal various aspects of His nature. So how do we display the supernatural in the natural world? Through the gifts He has placed in us! God designed us carefully and thoughtfully with gifts, and He reveals Himself through our natural world.

> God designed us carefully and thoughtfully with gifts, and He reveals Himself through our natural world.

Of course, no analogy can fully describe God, but the Scriptures speak about how His glory is often manifested as light:

The sun shall be no more
your light by day,
nor for brightness shall the moon
give you light;
but the LORD *will be your everlasting light,*
and your God will be your glory (Isaiah 60:19, ESV).

When Moses and Elijah came to the mountain to meet Jesus at the Transfiguration, Matthew described His glory as light:

And after six days Jesus took with him Peter and James,
and John his brother, and led them up a high mountain by
themselves. And he was transfigured before them, and his

face shone like the sun, and his clothes became white as light
(Matthew 17:1–2, ESV).

John also described God as light:

This is the message we have heard from him and proclaim
to you, that God is light, and in him is no darkness at all
(1 John 1:5, ESV).

Paul told Timothy that God lives in light:

. . . who alone is immortal and who lives in unapproachable
light . . . (1 Timothy 6:16, NIV).

Many times throughout Scripture, God shows His glory as
light (2 Corinthians 3:7–18, 2 Corinthians 4:4–5, Isaiah 58:8,
Isaiah 60:1).

If we imagine a beam of white light, most of what we see isn't
light itself. We see the effects the light has on the objects around it.
While we can easily see the effects, looking at the light itself, well,
that is something altogether different. What do you actually see
when you look at light? You can't really describe it. It's just light,
and it's bright. Because what we mainly see when light is present
isn't the light itself, but the light reflecting off objects.

But what happens when you shine a beam of light onto a
sparkling, multifaceted jewel, like a diamond or ruby? If you paid
attention during your school science class, you would say that
the light is *refracted*. You might even say, "I see rainbows!" That
statement may not be technically true, but we know that the
facets of a diamond affect the way we see the light. The structure
of the jewel bends the light waves, revealing layers we couldn't
see before. What we see as a beam of white light is really a whole
spectrum of colors.

God is like that white beam of light. And we are like the jewel God refracts the light through, making His many attributes visible to the world through our gifts. God's glorious qualities shine through our humanity. As the light strikes each individual facet of our God-given gifts, His glory shines.

Through the doctor, we see healing.

Through the teacher, we know nurturing.

Through the athlete, we witness precision and power.

Through the sculptor, we view a new creation.

Through the musician, we experience sounds and melodies that stir our innermost being.

However, many people are incredibly gifted, but they have never realized their gifts serve as a conduit to the supernatural world. Whether they know it or not, God's glory shines as they exhibit their gifts.

> *For since the creation of the world God's invisible qualities—his eternal power and divine nature—have been clearly seen, being understood from what has been made, so that men are without excuse (Romans 1:20, NIV).*

God has given incredible gifts to every person, even people outside the Body of Christ. He gave them in order to draw our attention to the great need we all have for Him. *Within* the Body of Christ, believers use their gifts to reveal even *more* about God. We use our gifts as tools to accomplish God's call for us as individuals. We also use them together in community to accomplish His ultimate goals. As we use our gifts to fulfill our divine purposes rather than our own, we show the world that something is higher, more important, and more worthy than the shallow earthly riches so many people run after. And as we grow to be more and more Christlike, and grow deeper in community and love with each other, we show the world more of who God is. In this way, we give people who need to see Christ a glimpse of the perfect relationship each member of the Trinity shares—that is the same kind of intimacy God invites us to share with Him.

If we could see each other as God sees us, we would be very surprised. We would find many people whom God has equipped to handle tasks quietly and spectacularly or given positions that we never considered for them. We would see them as unpolished jewels or wrapped-up gifts that they may not even know they possess!

If all members of the Church utilized their gifts to their full capacity, what would happen? If, instead of causing jealousy and spite, each person's gifts were recognized, encouraged, and developed by their brothers and sisters, what would it look like? It would create such a shining and outstanding community, full of talent, beauty, and godly character that you couldn't hide it, no matter how hard you tried! A community like that would be so different from the world's standards that outsiders wouldn't be able to stop looking on in wonder. Nonbelievers would be unable to deny that there's something different about us. They would find themselves drawn to us because they would see something otherworldly and supernatural about us. They would ask, "What is it in you that's so different, and why am I so drawn to it?"

11

The Glory

If I'm washing dishes I do it to the glory of God and if I pick up
a straw from the ground I do it for the glory of God.
　　　　　　　　　　　　　　　　　　　—Brother Lawrence

We need to have clarity about a very important word—
glory. I've been teaching about the glory of God for years.
It has captivated and fascinated me. It has made me a better
husband, father, and minister. Only recently did the Holy Spirit
reveal to me that there's more to God's glory than I originally
thought.

For years, I focused on one aspect of God's glory. It's not that
I've been completely unaware of other definitions and interpre-
tations of the word glory. I just didn't know exactly how they
applied to the other things I'm sharing with you. Finally,
I realized that all the other uses of this important word
throughout the Old and New Testaments actually work
together. They reveal the complete meaning and purpose of
the word. Like variables in a chemical equation, the uses of the
word "glory," when combined together, lead to an exponential
reaction that produces something very powerful: defined purpose. Christlikeness. True worship.

I remember my early exposure to the word *glory*. I remember sometimes in the church people used it as a "substitute" curse word or simply as an exclamation:

"Well, glory!"

"Glory to God . . . I got a raise!"

"Glory Hallelujah, thank you Jesus, amen!"

Maybe you grew up around people who said things like that. On the other hand, maybe you've heard the word used to describe a wonderful prayer meeting or worship service: "The glory of God showed up!" Whatever your experience is with the word, if you're like me, you were probably confused about its meaning. Is glory something God possesses? Is it something we declare? Do we often reserve it for God and the things that are super holy? Is it a cloud or a fog that rolls in during the slow songs at church? What is it?

In the Bible, the word *glory* has several broad meanings and applications. Most of the time, the word is used as a verb or a noun. In a few cases, the Bible uses it as an adverb and an adjective. For example:

And the priests could not enter the house of the LORD, *because the glory of the* LORD *had filled the* LORD's *house (2 Chronicles 7:2, NKJV).*

Let my mouth be filled with Your praise
And with Your glory all the day (Psalm 71:8, NKJV).

Therefore glorify the LORD *in the dawning light,*
The name of the LORD *God of Israel in the coastlands of the sea (Isaiah 24:15, NKJV).*

In that day the LORD *of hosts will be*
For a crown of glory and a diadem of beauty
To the remnant of His people (Isaiah 28:5, NKJV).

. . . for all have sinned and fall short of the glory of God (Romans 3:23, NKJV).

To them God willed to make known what are the riches of the glory of this mystery among the Gentiles: which is Christ in you, the hope of glory (Colossians 1:27, NKJV).

Let your light so shine before men, that they may see your good works and glorify your Father in heaven (Matthew 5:16, NKJV).

The Bible uses this word in many different ways. I will focus primarily on the verb and noun forms of the word, because those are the most common. In these forms, the Bible expresses the words used for glory in two ways (Papa, 2014, 25). The first is the most common use. In Hebrew, the word *kabowd* describes what I refer to as *inherent glory*. This definition of the word expresses the intrinsic character and nature of a person or thing—in this case, God. Moses used this word when he made a request to God: "Show me your glory" (Exodus 33:18).

A formal translation of *kabowd* means "heavy" or "weighty." That definition carries with it the idea of abundance, meaning that a lot of something is heavy. "It refers to the great physical weight or 'quantity' of a thing" (Vine, Unger, and White, 1996, 1:114). In this case, it means the weightiness of God—the substance of God. In my understanding, I'd say that *the glory of God is everything that makes God, God.*

It is everything that makes God who He is.

It is what makes up His character and nature.

It is *who* He is.

It is *inherent.*

It is His *inherent glory.*

The word *kabowd* has its roots in another Hebrew verb—*kabad.* This word means, "to make oneself dense" (Strong, 2001). It's similar to a term used primarily in physics and chemistry—mass.

Merriam-Webster's Dictionary defines mass as "the property of a body that is a measure of its inertia and that is commonly taken as a measure of the amount of material it contains and causes it to have weight in a gravitational field." That's a whole lot of words to explain that mass isn't actually the weight of something, it's a measurement of what a body contains—its density. When we refer to the *inherent glory* of God, it's like referring to the mass of God. It's *everything* God, but compacted, consolidated, or condensed into a manifestation that creation can experience. No wonder the Lord told Moses, "You cannot see my face and live" (Exodus 33:20)!

The authors of the Old Testament also used this word to describe the inherent glory in every human being (Exodus 28:2, Job 29:20, and Psalm 8:5, 30:11, 49:17). That tells me there's inherent value in every person, God's ultimate creation. Every created person has worth and importance. Though our glory isn't as "weighty" as the glory of God, this inherent glory does have purpose and meaning. I love how Thomas Carlyle put it: "Through every star, through every grass-blade, and most [of all] through every living soul, the glory of a present God still beams" (Ritzema and Vince, 2013).

We see the second use of the word "glory" is found in the New Testament with the Greek word *doxa*. Greek authors outside the New Testament used it to mean "opinion" or "reputation." The Septuagint (a Greek translation of the Hebrew Old Testament) replaces the Hebrew word *kabod* with the Greek word *doxa* (Nixon, 1996, 415). This word for glory is what I would like to call *expressed glory.*

Whether used as a noun or a verb, this is the kind of glory that *is given in response* to something or someone. Often, it is used to describe a *response to* inherent glory. It's often expressed by glorifying, giving glory to, or declaring the glory of someone or something. Much of what we describe as *worship* relates to this word for glory.

As you can see, this word "glory," as it's used throughout the Bible, varies some in its definition and use. Just as it's important to understand how each reagent works in a chemical reaction, I think we need to understand the different ways the Bible uses "glory" so we can get the full picture. Here's my definition of *glory*, based on the ways the Bible uses the word:

> The accurate opinion and measure of something's worth or value based on its intrinsic, indigenous, and innate qualities is its *inherent glory*.
>
> The revelation of this *inherent glory* results in the adoration, declaration, and exaltation of what has been revealed to us—*expressed glory*.
>
> *Put even more simply—we are created with the glory God gave to each person, and as we recognize God's glory, we give God glory.*

Not enough pages exist to develop a theology of God's glory, but I hope that I've cleared up the subject a little bit. We understand so little, and we still need to learn so much. We can only handle a little bit at a time. We can see the ways God decided to display some of His own glory—He painted a picture for us. Just walk outside at night, lift your head, and open your eyes:

> *The heavens proclaim the glory of God.*
> *The skies display his craftsmanship.*
> *Day after day they continue to speak;*
> *night after night they make him known.*
> *They speak without a sound or word;*
> *their voice is never heard.*
> *Yet their message has gone throughout the earth,*
> *and their words to all the world . . . (Psalm 19:1–4, NLT).*

Since before time began, everything has really been about God's glory. Each individual gift. Each person's purpose. Your dream. My dream. God designed all of these things to point us directly to Him. God wants all people to pursue Him, not only those who are unbelievers!

12

Created for Purpose

*If I find in myself a desire which no experience in this world
can satisfy, the most probable explanation is that I was made
for another world. If none of my earthly pleasures satisfy it,
that does not prove the universe is a fraud. Probably earthly
pleasures were never meant to satisfy it, but only to arouse it,
to suggest the real thing.*

—C. S. Lewis

Henry Ford. Thomas Edison. John Deere. Orville and
Wilbur Wright. Bill Gates. Steve Jobs. It would be a chal-
lenge to find someone who doesn't know these names. Why?
Because of the things they created, of course. Each of these men
became famous because of something they invented, but even
more because we *wanted to use* those inventions. These people
created things that met needs. Their creations satisfied a demand!
That's really why we know their names.

We remember the name Henry Ford, because many people
wanted to get from point A to point B through faster means
than a horse. We remember Thomas Edison because people
wanted all the modern wonders electricity made possible. We
remember Steve Jobs because he made it possible for you to
have a mobile phone, search the Internet, and send messages
on Twitter all at the same time (follow me @sionalford). We

celebrate these people as heroes, because each one of them created something that meets our needs. Their inventions satisfy
our desires.

Mark Kielburger, co-founder of Free the Children, said this:
"Gift + Issue = Change the World" (Kielburger, 2013). I like to say
it this way: God created and gifted you to solve a problem. God's
gift may not put you on the front cover of *Time Magazine* or *Sports
Illustrated*, but it can help the Body of Christ change the world.
Either God made you to reach one person at a time, or a stadium
of souls all at the same time, but He has given you a calling. Your
existence is proof of God's plan and purpose.

God never designed or created anything without purpose.

Never.

Myles Monroe said:

> Your existence is evidence that this generation needs
> something that your life contains. You are the creation that
> can meet God's desired result. In essence, there is something
> you came to this planet to do that the world needs in this
> generation. Your birth is evidence that your purpose is
> necessary (Munroe, 2000, 295–297).

God does desire results—He wants the world redeemed, and
He placed you and me here to help do that. He gave us the tools
(gifts) we need to get the job done. We are on this planet to fulfill a
purpose—*His purpose*. This news should excite you! Next time you
look in the mirror, remember that you are unique because God's
calling on your life is unique.

You are different because your purpose is different.

You are the *way* you are because of *why* you are (Munroe, 1992,
1635–1636).

You are the way you are because of why you are.

God gave you gifts to be the tools that will help you solve the problems He created you to resolve. He chose your purpose long before He created you to fulfill that purpose:

". . . I make known the end from the beginning,
   from ancient times, what is still to come.
I say, 'My purpose will stand,
   and I will do all that I please'" (Isaiah 46:10, NIV).

Think about this: He knows the end from the perspective of the beginning. He sees us fulfilling His purpose for us. He sees us walking in our destiny.

Then He creates.

Then He makes.

All good designers do this. For example, when the designer of my computer mouse began to design it, the purpose was already determined. It needed to fit on the front part of the main body of a laptop so it would be ergonomically accessible. It needed to be flat so that the laptop screen could fold down and close. It needed to be touch-sensitive and capable of interpreting multiple gestures. It needed areas to click left and right. The designer didn't begin designing this mouse until the purpose was clear. He didn't say, "I'll build a computer mouse and see where it fits!" No. The design followed the purpose.

Many people become frustrated because they try to fulfill a purpose the Creator didn't design them to fulfill. They try to solve problems God didn't create them to solve. So they're confused, frustrated, ineffective, inefficient, and unfulfilled.

So how do you discover your purpose? How can you know the purpose for which God made you?

First, you must connect with the Author—your Creator—and ask Him. No one knows the reason the Creator created something more intimately than the One who created it. God prearranged the end goal of everything He created. He knew your destination from the very beginning (Munroe, 1992, 1635-1636). That means he designed and created you:

> But the plans of the Lord stand firm forever,
>   the purposes of his heart through all generations
>   (Psalm 33:11, NIV).

> The purposes of a person's heart are deep waters,
>   but one who has insight draws them out (Proverbs 20:5, NIV).

It's simple. Find God and you will find your purpose. He made you. He designed you. He knows your end from your beginning. He knows your destination before you even start the journey. He has given you the gifts, the talents, the personality, and all the other necessary tools you need to complete the journey. He holds the blueprint.

Second, as you make your journey from the promise God gave to the promise fulfilled, you will discover your purpose. God will reveal your gifts and talents and help you sharpen them as you walk in His will. That's part of God's intent for your journey. That is one reason why God takes us on divine detours. And that's why you can't take a shortcut to the promise. You will need to take the long road. *No shortcuts.*

While you're on this journey, you will encounter many challenges and problems. Those challenges will stir your passion. Those problems may seem complicated and unsolvable to others, but you will have solutions that are obvious to you because God uniquely designed you to handle them. His desires and passions will actually become yours as you begin to discover your purpose. How? By delighting in Him. By pursuing Him and not the dream.

> Take delight in the Lord,
>   and he will give you the desires of your heart (Psalm 37:4, NIV).

It's time to take inventory. What do you love to do? What excites you and wakes you up early in the morning? What keeps you up late at night?

> What you love and desire to do naturally is probably what you were born to do, especially if those desires are given by God. Purpose allows you to be yourself. The discovery of purpose is the discovery of you (Munroe, 1992, 803-804).

I like that. Your discovery of purpose is the discovery of you.

God knows the end from the beginning (Isaiah 46:10), so He also knows every single need and has a solution for it. Great or small, God gave the answer in someone's purpose. The church must passionately express its love and adoration for God. God created psalmists (song-writers) and equipped them with a desire to compose songs for the church to sing. Homeless people need homes. So God created business people with a passion to help them by using their gifts as entrepreneurs to generate the funds to build houses. Sick people need comfort. So God created nurses and equipped them with compassion and mercy.

And the list goes on.

This is my point: When we like what someone has created or produced, we give glory to the creator of that thing (Giglio, 2012). An inventor receives well-deserved honor and gratitude. That inventor may even have a place in the history books because of a great creation that meets people's needs.

In short, when something fulfills its purpose, its creator is revealed and glorified. In the same way, when you fulfill your purpose, God is glorified. And when He is glorified, you will be satisfied.

In the same way, when you fulfill your purpose, God is glorified. And when He is glorified, you will be satisfied.

John Piper quotes Jonathan Edwards:

The manifestation of his own glory is the highest happiness of his creatures. Virtually everything I preach and write and do is shaped by this truth: that the exhibition of God's glory and the deepest joy of human souls are one thing (Piper quoting Edwards, 2013, 364-365).

When you use your God-given gifts, you will feel gratified, empowered, and enabled to do something beyond yourself. When you use that gift for its intended purpose, to display the holiness and beauty of God, you will receive deep, lasting satisfaction. And that brings glory to your Creator.

For me, I have that experience when I'm standing on a platform with a microphone in front of me, holding a guitar in my hands, and leading a congregation in worshipping our Creator. That's one of the most fulfilling things ever. Why? Because God created me to do it.

But it would not bring God glory if I were only concerned about standing on a stage. If I only played and sang for my own glory, I would never be satisfied; I would be desperately seeking another opportunity to glorify myself again, like an addict tries to feed an addiction. Self-glory only creates a deeper need for more glory, which is exactly what happened with Lucifer. However, if I use my gift to reveal the holiness and beauty of God, I feel deeply satisfied.

God created each of us to do different things. What did He create you to do? When do you have godly satisfaction? When do you feel that the work you're doing isn't a task or a duty, but rather a *burden?* Is it when you're writing? Could it be when you're painting, sculpting, or cooking? Perhaps it's when you're walking through a particularly bitter struggle with a close friend or battling for that friend in prayer.

I also experience divine fulfillment when I check on my children at night. I quietly open their bedroom doors after they have gone to sleep. I look down at their peaceful faces and a feeling just comes over me. A heart pang and deep desire washes over me, and I feel moved to pray like never before. It's something God created me to do—to be a father to my children and a husband to my wife. And nothing I ever do, say, or buy can ever satisfy me like fulfilling that purpose.

I recently met a couple while I watched my oldest son play in a baseball tournament. My wife and I had been at the ballpark all day, baking under the hot Texas sun. Beside me sat this wonderful, elderly couple. Through the course of conversation, I discovered that they had never missed even *one* of their grandson's baseball games! Even though their grandson was one of *seven* grandchildren. I asked the husband why he bothered to drive four hundred miles (two hundred miles each way) every weekend just to see his grandson play ball. He answered with deep conviction:

All my life we've raised our kids. We struggled through many things couples struggle through during forty-eight years of marriage. But this is our calling. Nothing fulfills me more than watching these kids do what they love. It is a blessing and brings so much satisfaction.

Their incredible passion really convicted me once again about callings, dreams, and purposes. God is infinitely creative, and each of us has different gifts and different dreams.

Unfortunately, many people, including Christians, feel that if they don't climb the ladder of success and knock down someone above them, they'll never feel fulfilled. Many people don't know what it means to be satisfied like that elderly couple I met. Instead of contentment, they feel a constant hunger, an emptiness they can't define.

If you are one of those people, don't worry. I wrote this book to help you come to the place where you *know* what God created you to do, because when you know and you do that thing, you'll experience contentment like you never thought possible. Look at what God says in His Word:

> "They are my own people,
> and I created them to bring me glory" (Isaiah 43:7, GNT).

Remember, God created you to glorify Him! You can know that is the *one* purpose at the center of your being, including everything He's given you and everything He calls you to do. Whatever else you may choose to do with your gifts might be wonderful, but those things are secondary to your ultimate purpose. The truth is that you will be most satisfied and He will be most glorified when you're using your gifts to bring Him glory.

> "The happiness of the creature consists in rejoicing in God, by which also God is magnified and exalted." But I also love to say it my way: God is most glorified in us when we are most satisfied in him.
>
> —John Piper

> You are created to glorify your Creator through the productivity of your works. Therefore, glorifying God is not limited to praising Him, but rather to putting your hand to productive, wholesome, and positive work.
>
> —Myles Munroe

13

Show Me the Glory

Show me Thy glory, I pray Thee, that so I may know Thee indeed.
—*A. W. Tozer*

This verse in the Bible has always fascinated me:

> *Then Moses said, "Now show me your glory" (Exodus 33:18, NIV).*

Moses' request tells me something significant—there really is a big difference between God's presence and God's glory. Moses had experienced God's presence by witnessing a manifestation of God's presence, God's *Shekinah*. (Brand, England, Bond, Clenenden, and Butler, 2003). Moses had discarded his sandals and stood on holy ground (Exodus 3:5). He had been to the Israelites "the tent of meeting," where Moses spoke with God just as a man speaks with his friend (Exodus 33:11). Moreover, he had seen what God produces through His power, when God sent ten plagues upon Egypt (Exodus 7–11) and parted the Red Sea so the Israelites could escape from an angry Egyptian army (Exodus 14). However, Moses wanted more. More of God.

Moses had experienced the *presence* of God, now he wanted to experience the *person* of God. Moses knew there was a difference

between God's presence and God's glory. Moreover, Moses wanted
to see that difference. He wanted to see behind the veil to the *source*
of God's presence. He didn't want only to see what God could do;
he wanted God Himself—everything that makes God who He is.
He wanted to see the *kabowd*—God's *glory*.

> Moses had experienced the
> *presence* of God, now he wanted
> to experience the *person* of God.

Of course, God is everywhere—He's omnipresent. He is right
here with me now. He's with me when I drive to work. He is with
me when I stand behind the pulpit at church. In addition, He's even
with me when I stand in line to buy something at a store. God's
presence is everywhere.

However, God's glory is not always *omni-manifested*. I made up
that word, but it makes sense. We don't always see it. God must
manifest or reveal His glory for us to experience it. Until He reveals
it, He conceals it. Hidden from our senses. Hidden until He
makes it known. Yes, His glory is always there, but it's not always
apparent and visible.

Sometimes we talk about the glory of God and say it is the
"manifested presence of God." While I understand this definition
is true, it falls short of fully describing God's glory. For example,
if a man walked into a busy office where you work and sat down
at a desk behind you, his presence would be with you. You would
both occupy the same room, sharing space with him and the
other people working in the room. You may not have even noticed
when he walked in. You might not recognize him. Still, he is
there—present.

After a few minutes, someone else in the room recognizes the
man and reveals that he isn't simply another employee at a desk.

He is the owner and president of the company! Now, you look a little closer and realize that you recognize him from the company website. That's him—and he is here! Now, you don't simply think of him as being present in the room. Everyone there recognizes him *and* he is in the room! That's what I mean when I say, manifested *presence*. He may have been there the entire time, but now, you definitely recognize him.

Similarly, God is omnipresent, and you still may not recognize Him. He is in your home, your place of work, your church's worship service—yet we all fail to recognize Him sometimes. However, when we do, He is with us, and He manifests His presence. He's not more present than he was before. Instead, we recognize His presence. That is *manifest presence*. Myles Monroe explained it this way:

> Presence means "pre-sense"; we get a "sense" of God before He fully manifests Himself. The presence of God is His predetermined environment for us to function and be fruitful. The glory of God, on the other hand, is the attributes and character of God on display (Munroe, 2000, 34).

Continuing the example of the company president—although he is in the room and everyone is now aware, he hasn't revealed who he really is to everyone. Some of the people only know *about* him. They know he occupies an important position in the company. They know he has authority and power, but they don't *know* him. They don't know his character or his virtue. They will only know these things when he meets and reveals himself personally to each individual in the room. So he starts by sitting down across from every person and speaking with them privately. He opens up his wallet and shows you pictures of his grandchildren. He shares with you the story of when he and his wife met forty years ago. He explains that he never graduated from college, because he returned home to take care of his widowed mother after his father died. Now, you're really getting to know him. He is revealing himself and his character—who he really is—to you.

So when Moses had a conversation with the Owner of the Universe in Exodus 33, he began to know God's character and virtue. Moses approached God with a contrite heart and a thirst for God's presence, and God revealed Himself. Moses didn't want to go to God's Promised Land without the God of Promise:

> And he [the Lord] said, "My presence will go with you, and I will give you rest." And he [Moses] said to him, "If your presence will not go with me, do not bring us up from here. For how shall it be known that I have found favor in your sight, I and your people? Is it not in your going with us, so that we are distinct, I and your people, from every other people on the face of the earth?" And the Lord said to Moses, "This very thing that you have spoken I will do, for you have found favor in my sight, and I know you by name" (Exodus 33:14–17, ESV).

Then, Moses' next sentence may be the boldest thing any human has ever spoken:

> "Now, since I have found favor in your eyes and you know me by name . . . show me Your glory" (Exodus 33:18; paraphrased).

If the heaven's angels were watching, I'm guessing their jaws dropped. A holy hush probably fell over all creation as all eyes fixed on the conference between the Great I AM and His great ambassador. How would God answer this brave request?

> And the Lord said, "I will cause all my goodness to pass in front of you, and I will proclaim my name, the Lord, in your presence.

I will have mercy on whom I will have mercy, and I will have
compassion on whom I will have compassion. But," he said, "you
cannot see my face, for no one may see me and live" (Exodus
33:19–20, NIV).

God answered with mercy and compassion. God said, "Yes,
but . . ." God could not allow Moses to see the entirety of His glory,
because it would be fatal for any sinful creature to see the full glory
of God. In the Bible, several people receive limited manifestations of
God's glory. However, seldom does God fully manifest Himself.
When He does, the results are both spectacular and terrifying. For
example; the mountains caught on fire (Exodus 19, Deuteronomy
4:11–13), people who were not covered died (2 Samuel 6:7), and on
one occasion 50,070 people perished when several unaware and
very ignorant farmers opened up the Ark of God at Beth Shemesh
(1 Samuel 6:19).

So how does the all-powerful, omnipotent God reveal Himself
to people if it will kill us? God has the ability to conceal and show
His glory, both at the same time. He shows Himself in small, measured portions:

You have not come to a mountain that can be touched and that
is burning with fire; to darkness, gloom and storm; to a trumpet
blast or to such a voice speaking words that those who heard it
begged that no further word be spoken to them, because they
could not bear what was commanded: "If even an animal touches
the mountain, it must be stoned to death." The sight was so
terrifying that Moses said, "I am trembling with fear."
But you have come to Mount Zion, to the city of the living
God, the heavenly Jerusalem. You have come to thousands
upon thousands of angels in joyful assembly, to the church of the
firstborn, whose names are written in heaven. You have come to
God, the Judge of all, to the spirits of the righteous made perfect,

to Jesus the mediator of a new covenant, and to the sprinkled
blood that speaks a better word than the blood of Abel (Hebrews
12:18–24, NIV).

I love that God didn't rebuke Moses. In God's infinite mercy, He understood Moses' request. He saw the purity and passion of Moses' heart. God saw a man who passionately pursued Him behind the cloud. He saw a broken, humble leader who wanted a more intimate relationship with Him.

Would that describe you? Do you want the presence of God more than you want the promise of God?

14

Hidden in the Rock

After all my years of Bible study, seminary training, preaching,
and teaching, and after all the books I have read, I have come
to the conclusion and conviction that nothing is more important
than the glory of God.

—*Myles Monroe*

I love Key Lime Pie. In case you don't know what that is, it's a
delicious dessert first made in Florida. It has Key lime juice, egg
yolks, and sweetened condensed milk. Then the cook puts it all in
a piecrust. Delicious! If you know where I live, go ahead and send
one my way.

Several years ago, I took a friend to dinner at one of my favorite
seafood restaurants. I had just finished the main course, when the
server asked us if we would like dessert. "Our special today is Key
Lime Pie. Would you like one?"

"Does a cat have climbing gear?" I replied. "Yes!"

A few minutes later, she arrived at our table with a small plate
and a "sliver" of Key Lime Pie. I politely joked with her that I
wanted a *whole* Key Lime *Pie*, not a *piece* of Key lime pie!

"Could you bring me the container this came out of?" I teased.

She had not brought a Key Lime Pie, only *part* of the whole
pie. In some ways, that's how God reveals His glory to us. We can't

handle all of it, so He gives us "slices" of His glory so we can see it and not be killed by the power of it.

If I ate an entire Key Lime Pie, it wouldn't be a healthy thing to do. Believe me, I've tried it, and the results were not good! The same is true with God's glory. He knows we can't take a full dose of His glory, so He reveals Himself to us in smaller, bite-sized revelations.

God really showed mercy and compassion by honoring Moses' request, but with a slight change:

"But," he said, "you cannot see my face, for no one may see me and live" (Exodus 33:20, NIV).

The word for "face" used here in the Hebrew text means "in front of, forward, before, in the presence of, or in the face of" (Strong, 2015). God was telling Moses, "You cannot see the front, the forward area, the face of My presence—or it will kill you!"

So how was Moses supposed to see the glory of Yahweh, the Eternal One? Here was God's plan:

Then the Lord said, "There is a place near me where you may stand on a rock" (Exodus 33:21, NIV).

In order for Moses to experience God's glory, he first had to go to a place near God and stand on a rock. We must do something very similar if we want to experience God's glory and become vessels of it. If you want God to use you to display His glory, you first must position yourself on the rock near the source of glory—God. Jesus reminds us that we must not only hear God's words, but we must also put them into practice if we want to build our lives on solid ground:

"Therefore everyone who hears these words of mine and puts them into practice is like a wise man who built his house on the rock. The rain came down, the streams rose, and the winds

*blew and beat against that house; yet it did not fall, because
it had its foundation on the rock. But everyone who hears
these words of mine and does not put them into practice is
like a foolish man who built his house on sand. The rain
came down, the streams rose, and the winds blew and
beat against that house, and it fell with a great crash"*
(Matthew 7:24–27, NIV).

Later, when Jesus asked His disciples who they believed that
He was, everyone but Simon muttered things they had heard
about Jesus. Simon had a different response. Simon shared his
own personal revelation of *who* Jesus was. He declared, "You are
the Messiah, the Son of the living God" (Matthew 16:16, NIV).
Jesus then responded to Peter's revelation by saying:

*And I tell you that you are Peter, and on this rock I will
build my church, and the gates of Hades will not overcome it*
(Matthew 16:18, NIV).

Stand on the rock. Draw near to God, and He will draw near
to you (James 4:8). Don't just hear the words of God, obey them
(James 1:22–25). The rock is the place where God reveals His true
character and virtue. Stand on it. Build on it.

Now, back to Exodus 33:

*Then the Lord said, "There is a place near me where you may
stand on a rock. When my glory passes by, I will put you in a
cleft in the rock and cover you with my hand until I have passed
by. Then I will remove my hand and you will see my back; but
my face must not be seen"* (Exodus 33:21–23, NIV).

God will position you for encounters with His glory. Notice, *God*
placed Moses in the crevice or cleft in the rock. In much the same
way, God positions *us* according to our callings and our gifts to look

on His glory from strategic positions. It's very important to realize we can't acquire these positions through our own efforts or elbowing our way to the top; they come through surrender and humility. Please don't miss the significance of God's involvement in our positioning. He knows exactly where to place us so we can behold and experience the manifestation of His glory. And it doesn't stop there. Glory beheld becomes glory revealed—glory that we behold today will be the same glory we reveal to others tomorrow.

> Glory beheld becomes glory revealed—
> glory that we behold today will be the
> same glory we reveal to others tomorrow.

God also doesn't place us in just any rock; He places us in *the* Rock—Jesus. He is the Rock to whom we run. He is the shelter and fortress where we hide from storms (Psalm 27:5). The river of life flows from this Rock, and it is the source and the supply of life (1 Corinthians 10:4). Moreover, from this vantage point, where we are hidden in Christ, we behold His glory (John 1:17) and we reveal His glory:

> *For you died, and your life is now hidden with Christ in God. When Christ, who is your life, appears, then you also will appear with him in glory (Colossians 3:3–4, NIV).*

Do you want to appear with Jesus in glory? Do you want to experience and reveal God's glory? Do you want the gifts that He has given you to be vessels through which He displays His glory to the world? If so, think about three points that we've discovered from Moses' encounter with God:

1. If you want to experience God's glory, you must draw near to Him and stand on the firm rock of His Word.

2. God positions you to encounter His glory according to your callings and gifts. So surrender your life to Him and walk in obedience to His Word.

3. God places you in the safe Rock of Jesus so that you'll be hidden in Christ and positioned to experience a revelation of His glory. So allow Him to hide you, sometimes in places of obscurity and mystery.

15

Glory Revealed

The smiling face of God is always turned toward us—but the cloud of concealment is of our own making.

—*A. W. Tozer*

Have you ever met face-to-face with a famous person? Have you ever seen a famous person on a crowded street or in a busy shopping area? Most of them don't really want to stand out. If anything, they try to blend in with their surroundings so that no one will recognize them. They usually prefer to be unnoticed and unbothered.

At an event, I recently encountered Tony Stewart, a top NASCAR driver. I was standing in a behind-the-scenes area of a local racetrack when he stepped out of a doorway right in front of me. I love auto racing, so I almost wanted to hug him, tell him my name, and let him know what a huge fan I am. However, I could see by the look on his face that he was silently saying, "Please don't recognize me!" Therefore, I didn't bother him. I just gave him a casual greeting and kept walking.

If you really want to see some famous people, one of the best places to spot them is the airport, especially in Atlanta, New York, Nashville, or Los Angeles. I've been to all of these airports and seen some famous, trying-to-hide people. They usually wear hats and sunglasses, which makes them easy to pick out of a crowd. They hide their face, because their identity is in their face.

When Moses asked to see God's glory, he wanted to see God's famous face behind the veil, those features that made God recognizable. He had spoken to God "face to face, as one speaks to a friend" (Exodus 33:11, NIV), but he wanted to *see* that face. He wanted to see his Creator.

So why was this time different from any of the other times Moses spoke face to face with God? If it would kill him now, why didn't it kill him earlier? It's because Moses had never seen God's face. He had only spoken to him face to face. In all of Moses' previous encounters with the God of glory, there was always smoke, a cloud, or a veil hiding God's face. Moses had never actually seen the face of God; he had only heard His voice.

> Then the Lord said, "There is a place near me where you may stand on a rock. When my glory passes by, I will put you in a cleft in the rock and cover you with my hand until I have passed by. Then I will remove my hand and you will see my back; but my face must not be seen." (Exodus 33:21–23, NIV).

As I mentioned earlier, God allowed Moses to see Him in this special encounter, but God placed Moses in a place where God's hand would protect him in the crevice of a rock. God's glory and His face passed by, and at the last second, God removed His hand and allowed Moses to view God's back.

So God has a back? Yes, though it's probably not what we picture. The word used for "back" here is 'hōrāy. One commentary describes the back of God by saying, "Since God is Spirit and has no form, and since no one can see Him and live, the word 'hōrāy could just as well and more accurately be rendered 'the aftereffects' of His radiant glory, which had just passed by" (Kaiser, 1990, 2:484). God allowed Moses to see the "after-effects" of His glory. Alternatively, as I like to say, Moses was able to see the *history* of God. Moses saw the remnants of God's present glory and the fullness of His past glory.

I don't know, but I think it's *possible* that this revelation of God's backside contained the "history" of God's glory, and so Moses was able to author the first five books of the Bible under the inspiration of the Spirit of God.

Could this encounter be why Moses was able to write the Genesis account of creation? Could this be the reason he was able to describe the historical accounts of everything that happened before humans were around to write it down? I don't know, but I think it's *possible* that this revelation of God's backside contained the "history" of God's glory, and so Moses was able to author the first five books of the Bible under the inspiration of the Spirit of God.

I could say many things about this meeting, but I want to emphasize something important for our discussion of the glory of God. Remember when Moses asked God to "show me Your glory?" God's reply was "I will pass all of My goodness before you and I will proclaim My name in your presence." God reveals His glory to us in two remarkable ways: all of His goodness *and* the proclamation of His name. We've discussed the "goodness" side of this manifestation in detail, but what about the other side—the proclamation of His name?

The proclamation of God's name is a declaration of His authority over everything. In addition, whenever God's name is present and declared, God's supreme and sovereign dominion is established. One commentary says:

This was a sermon on the name of the Lord that disclosed
to Moses the most hidden nature of Jehovah. It proclaimed
that God is love, but that kind of love in which mercy, grace,
long-suffering, goodness, and truth are united with holiness
and justice. (Keil and Delitzsch, 1996, 1:478).

God proclaimed and declared His name to Moses in this way.
In Moses' first encounter with God at the burning bush, Moses
asked, "Who shall I say sent me?" God answered: "Tell them I AM
sent you" (Exodus 13:14). This first revelation of God's name to
humanity didn't disappear with His revelation on Mount Sinai;
instead, it brought additional depth and clarity. Most biblical
scholars think we can't really know how to pronounce God's
name. In fact, such fear surrounded mentioning His name that
the Jewish community prohibited anyone saying it aloud. Only
the high priest could say it, and only once per year on the Day of
Atonement.

The Creator gave a glimpse of His DNA to Moses. He exposed
every facet of Himself to Moses—everything He contained—all in
one moment. God revealed more than the *Shekinah* that I mentioned earlier. God revealed more than He had at a burning bush
in the wilderness (Exodus 3:1–3). God revealed all of Himself to a
mortal man.

Whenever we ask to see God's glory, we must prepare to
accept His full authority and dominion in our lives. Wherever
His name is declared, His judgment accompanies it and He
makes known His mercy. It's a package deal. With these words,
God described His own character and virtue: loving, merciful,
kind, compassionate, gracious, patient, faithful, and forgiving.
Moses knew every one of them.

God's justice is also an essential part of His nature. He authori-
tatively declared this fact to Moses when He said, "Yet he does not
leave the guilty unpunished; he punishes the children and their

children for the sin of the parents to the third and fourth generation" (Exodus 34:7b, NIV). Whenever God reveals His glory to
us, even in part, we experience His goodness and His Lordship.
We can't have one without the other. We all are quick to embrace
the goodness of God, but we must also be willing to accept His
Lordship in our lives. Where He reveals His glory, His mercy and
grace are present, but His judgment is also near.

> Where He reveals His glory, His mercy and
> grace are present, but His judgment is also near.

Be careful when you ask God to "Show us Your glory." When
His goodness and name are proclaimed in our midst, things can die
and die quickly. Glory disclosed means that God delays His judgment. In other words, when His glory is present, judgment is near.

16

Glory Comes with Holiness

No attribute of God is more dreadful to sinners than His holiness.
—Matthew Henry

What makes God's glory so powerful and even deadly? Why is the display of God's goodness dangerous itself? Why would the proclamation of His name bring judgment and destruction to some people?

One word: *holiness*.

I've spent nearly all of my Christian life with a false understanding of God's holiness and my holiness. I've had the presumption that holiness meant perfection. I thought the more holy something was, the more perfect and cleaner it had to be. I equated holy with perfection. To me, holiness came with a rigid list of Dos and Don'ts:

Don't listen to that or you won't be holy.
Don't watch that or you won't be holy.
Wear your hair this way to be holy.
Wear this type of clothing and you'll be holy.
This verse only added to my derangement about the subject:
But just as he who called you is holy, so be holy in all you do; for it is written: "Be holy, because I am holy" (1 Peter 1:15–16, NIV).

That is a very strong command! *Be holy*. Why? "Because I am holy," said God! Thanks a lot, God. Now I have to be *perfect*?

How can I ever be perfect? God is perfect. Blameless. Very pure and without sin. I'm supposed to be this way as well? Does He actually mean that? Maybe He means that I need to work harder to be this way throughout my life. Maybe it's more of a lifelong goal than it is a present command.

If you've ever had similar thoughts, then maybe, like me, you haven't really understood the concepts of holiness, sanctification, and consecration. I know those are extremely religious-sounding words. Here's an example that may make things clearer:

The book of Joshua contains a story about the time when God commanded Joshua to lead the children of Israel into the Promised Land to possess it. The Israelites had wandered in the wilderness for forty years until the last of the men who were of fighting age when they left Egypt had died. Because of their disobedience, God did not let an entire generation enter into His promise. Now, the people were ready. They could see the Promised Land only a few miles away, just over the Jordan River.

Do you know what Joshua's orders were to his young army? Did he give them a rousing pep talk about being strong and brave in the face of battle? Or did he ride in on horseback, with his face painted as he shouted "freedom"?

No. Instead, he said something that sounded very "religious":

Joshua told the people, "Consecrate yourselves, for tomorrow the Lord will do amazing things among you" (Joshua 3:5, NIV).

Consecrate? Ouch.

The word used here for "consecrate" is *quadash*. It simply means, "to be set apart" (Strong, 2001). It appears in the Old Testament ninety-two times, and many times it's translated into words like consecrate, sanctify, holy, cleansed, hallow, or sacred. In this verse, it means, "to be set apart unto the Lord for special service." Or, in other words, "to make holy."

The Old Testament authors used two additional words in Hebrew for consecration: *nazir* and *nezer*. These words don't appear as often as *quadash* (just six out of the ninety-two instances), but they carry an important implication. Though the words also mean, "to be set apart," they're primarily used in a context that means, "to be set apart *from* something unto God" (Leviticus 21:12, Numbers 6:18–19), whereas *quadash* means, "to be set apart *unto* God."

Big difference.

In his book, *The Pleasure of His Company: A Journey to Intimate Friendship With God*, Dutch Sheets describes the difference between these words:

> The key to truly understanding God's heart in the use of *qadash* is the "unto Him" aspect. Though we have made sanctification and consecration religious and legalistic, they are actually relational concepts. A poor understanding of this has hindered our connection to Him. Consecration is for connection. In the same way that the wedding vow is relational, so is spiritual sanctification (Sheets, 2014, 2436–2466).

He also says that another Old Testament word for "holy" is *qodesh*. It comes from the root word *quadash*. When God calls us to be holy, He isn't simply calling us to be separate "*from* sin," rather He wants us to be separated "*unto* God."

Holiness is not about being *sinless*.
It is about being *separate*.

To summarize, holiness is not about being *sinless*. It is about being *separate*. When we live a life of separateness unto God, the natural result is separation from things that aren't of God. God is asking us to *this* kind of holiness:

Therefore,

> *"Come out from them*
> *and be separate,*
> *says the Lord.*
> *Touch no unclean thing,*
> *and I will receive you."*

And,

> *"I will be a Father to you,*
> *and you will be my sons and daughters,*
> *says the Lord Almighty"* (2 Corinthians 6:17–18, NIV).

God is not calling us to be separate *from* unclean things. Instead, He wants us to separate ourselves *unto* Him. Intimacy. True worship. Relationship. Our focus isn't to "not seek" sin. Our focus is to seek God. "*Qadash*, separation unto Him, is the cause; *qodesh*, holiness, is the effect" (Sheets, 2014, 2473–2474).

When we reorient our minds to understand the reality of holiness, we seek to connect with God instead of focusing on running from sin. Our aim becomes a relationship instead of a religious form or function. Our goal is *Him*, not an outward form of holiness, which is superficial and legalistic.

Now that we have a basic understanding of holiness, how does this apply to God's glory? I started this chapter by stating God's holiness makes His glory powerful and life changing. Again, holiness is separateness and otherness unto God or from something. How can this apply to God? How can God separate Himself from anything in order to be holy? The fact that He is God means He is already standing apart from everything else. So how can God separate Himself unto Himself when He already is Himself? Maybe that's why when Moses asked: "Who shall I say sent me," God answered by saying, "Tell them I AM sent you" (Exodus 3:13–14).

One time, I heard a preacher say that I AM means, "*You* are not." I would add to that and say I AM means, "You are not, and neither is anything that you can compare Him to!"

He is other. Separate. Incomparable. Unequaled. Superior. Superlative. Infinitely unique. Matchless. Unparalleled. Do you get the point?

Matt Papa explains it like this:

God's holiness is not so much an attribute of God as it is the foundation of all his attributes. It is Him (Papa, 2014, 41).

In addition, John Piper says:

[Holiness] is his infinite worth. His holiness is his utterly unique divine essence, which in his uniqueness has infinite value. It determines all that he is and does and is determined by no one. His holiness is what he is as God, which no one else is or ever will be. (Piper, 2013, 429–430).

These attributes could have remained a mystery, hidden from creation forever, but God chose to reveal them. He chose to put His holiness on display. This is the glory of God.

Piper continues:

The glory of God is the manifestation of his holiness. God's holiness is the incomparable perfection of his divine nature; his glory is the display of that holiness (Piper, 2013, 436–437).

God's holiness is a secret until His glory reveals it. His glory is
the manifestation of His holiness. That's why the angels cried out:
"Holy, Holy, Holy is the Lord of Hosts.

> God's holiness is a secret until His glory reveals it.
> His glory is the manifestation of His holiness.

The whole earth is filled with His *glory*"—because the description of God's holiness is infinite.

> "The whole earth is filled with His grace, His mercy, His
> compassion, His love, His healing, His kindness . . . ."
> (*15 minutes later*) "His generosity, His forgiveness, His
> creativity, His . . . ."
> (*1 year later*) "His wisdom, His awesomeness, His . . . ."
> (*100 years later*) "His grandeur, His majesty, His devotion,
> His . . . ."
> (*10,000 years later*) "His excellence, His purity, His . . . ."

Do you get the point? The angels could continue describing God's
holiness forever. That's why they simply said *glory*. Because it is
everything that makes God . . . God. It is His holiness revealed. Just
how vast and great is this glory? If God could give us some clue as
to how holy He is and how His attributes are without end, how
would He do it?

> *The heavens declare the glory of God;*
> *the skies proclaim the work of his hands (Psalm 19:1, NIV).*

If someone asks, "If earth is the only inhabited planet and man
the only rational inhabitant among the stars, why such a large
and empty universe?" The answer is: It's not about us. It's about

God. And that's an understatement. God created us to know him and love him and show him. And then he gave us a hint of what he is like —the universe (Piper, 2013, 494–496).

Vast. Without end. Inexhaustible. Infinite. Timeless.

How does this apply to you and me? We are part of the manifestation of God's glory. God created us *for* His glory:

> *"I will say to the north, 'Give them up!'*
> *and to the south, 'Do not hold them back.'*
> *Bring my sons from afar*
> *and my daughters from the ends of the earth—*
> *everyone who is called by my name,*
> *whom I created for my glory,*
> *whom I formed and made" (Isaiah 43:6–7, NIV).*

God made you *for* His glory. He purposefully created you to show forth His glory. He made us "in His image" (Genesis 1:27) so that the world could get a taste of Him, an *image* of Him. They could get a glimpse of who He is.

17

Glory Containers

If all the light of the heavenly luminaries had been contracted into one (light), it would have been destructive, not useful, to our sight; but being by divine wisdom distributed into sun, moon, and stars, each giving out his own proportion, it is suited to declare the glory of God and to enlighten the world. So, if the whole revelation of the glory of Christ, and all that belongs unto it, had been committed into one series and contexture of words, it would have overwhelmed our minds rather than enlightened us. (That is) why God has distributed the light of it through the whole firmament of the books of the Old and New Testament; whence it communicates itself, by various parts and degrees, unto the proper use of the church.

—John Owen

Again, God's glory is everything that makes God, God. It is His holiness revealed. It is His divine nature. His attributes. His character on display for all to see.

How does this really take effect? Look at Isaiah 6 again:

> And one [Seraph] cried to another and said:
> "Holy, holy, holy is the LORD of hosts;
> The whole earth is full of his glory!" (Isaiah 6:3, NKJV).

According to the angels in Isaiah's vision, the whole earth is full of God's glory. So where exactly is His glory? I've never seen the *Shekinah* glow mentioned in the Old Testament. Yet the *whole earth is full* of the glory of the Lord. According to the apostle Paul, the reason we don't see it comes from a big problem—Satan's deceit has obscured or veiled God's glory:

> *In their case the god of this world has blinded the minds of the unbelievers, to keep them from seeing the light of the gospel of the glory of Christ, who is the image of God (2 Corinthians 4:4, ESV).*

Satan actively works in this world, attempting to blind every person to the glory of God so they will remain captive to sin and darkness. Nevertheless, God wants to reveal His glory to us and, according to Habakkuk, He will accomplish His goal. At some time in the future:

> *For the earth will be filled*
> *with the knowledge of the glory of the Lord*
> *as the waters cover the sea (Habakkuk 2:14, ESV).*

Habakkuk's prophetic word was that the earth would be filled with the *knowledge* of the glory of the Lord. Isaiah 6 says that His glory already fills the earth. Nevertheless, His glory still needs to be revealed. The word *knowledge* in Habakkuk is so important, because it punctuates the promise of a time coming when the glory that is already in the earth will be recognized and revealed to all creation.

The word for "knowledge" used in this verse is *yada*, and it means, "to make known, to make oneself known, reveal" (Strong, 2001). When something is revealed, it means that it has been present all along. People did not perceive or recognize it.

It needed to be revealed.

There needed to be a *revelation* of God's glory—a *yada* of His nature, character, and attributes. A time is coming when the glory of God that is already in the earth will be revealed to the whole earth as the waters cover the sea. This promise sounds like a serious revival!

> A time is coming when the glory of God that is already in the earth will be revealed to the whole earth as the waters cover the sea. This promise sounds like a serious revival!

But wait. *As the waters cover the sea?*

Why does Habakkuk say this? Moreover, why did Isaiah say something very similar?

> *They will neither harm nor destroy*
>   *on all my holy mountain,*
> *for the earth will be filled with the knowledge of the Lord*
>   *as the waters cover the sea* (Isaiah 11:9, NIV).

What do these prophets mean when they say, "... as the waters cover the sea"? Several years ago, I asked the Holy Spirit to explain this concept to me. This is what I heard: *Water can be without a sea, but a sea cannot be without water.* The sea is a result of *many* waters joined together. There are billions of "waters" on the earth today. However, in a spiritual sense, the prophet means those "waters" that are you and me. Every human being. God created us to be His conduits, to reflect Him. The great revival that is coming will occur when all the "waters" come together and make a "sea" of glory!

That sounds like the Church to me. The real Church. The Body of Christ. That sounds like revival. You and I can be without the

Body of Christ, but the Body of Christ cannot be without us. It is the sum of many parts (you, me, and every other believer) like the ocean is the sum of many parts (all the bodies of water).

You and I can be without the Body of Christ, but the Body of Christ cannot be without us.

Jesus came to earth in the fullness of God's glory. He *was* God's glory, represented in human flesh. The Gospel of John says:

> *And the Word became flesh and dwelt among us, and we have seen his glory, glory as of the only Son from the Father, full of grace and truth (John 1:14, ESV).*

This description speaks about the arrival of God's glory *on* the earth. Jesus—Divinity wrapped in human flesh. Jesus made fresh footprints on the soil of the very planet He spoke into being. The glory of God was now also *in* earth. He was *in* human flesh. The Second Adam then gave birth to a multitude of Adams. Even more, because of that, you and I now get to be the Body of Christ—a representation of His fullness on the earth:

> *Now you are the body of Christ, and each one of you is a part of it (1 Corinthians 12:27, NIV).*

Now we are what Peter describes as:

> *. . . you yourselves like living stones are being built up as a spiritual house, to be a holy priesthood, to offer spiritual sacrifices acceptable to God through Jesus Christ (1 Peter 2:5, ESV).*

In addition, Paul says in Ephesians:

> . . . in whom the whole structure, being joined together, grows
> into a holy temple in the Lord. In him you also are being
> built together into a dwelling place for God by the Spirit
> (Ephesians 2:21–22, ESV).

Here, now, is our situation:

1. God's glory fills the whole earth.
2. Satan's deluding presence has obscured God's glory.
3. To see the full glory of God would prove fatal to sinful humans.
4. Some day in the future, "the whole earth will be filled with the
   knowledge of God's glory." Something dramatic, something
   revelatory, will happen to enable everyone to see God's glory.

In the meantime, before the fulfillment of Habakkuk 2:14, God's
people will reveal His glory:

> For God, who said, "Let light shine out of darkness,"
> made his light shine in our hearts to give us the light of
> the knowledge of the glory of God in the face of Christ
> (2 Corinthians 4:6, NIV).

Read that verse again slowly.

God has made His light shine in our hearts to give us "the light
of the knowledge of the glory of God in the face of Christ"! Paul
didn't say that God would one day shine His light into our hearts; he
said God's light is already shining in our hearts. When a light shines
into something, the source of the light is external, but when a light
shines in something, the source of the light is within! Do you know
what that means? God's glory is in you!

I used to read that verse in a very different way. I used to read it
and think, "God shined His light into my heart to reveal the ugliness

of my sin." However, that's all wrong! The truth is *so much bigger* than that. God has put His light *inside* of us. He put His glory— everything that makes God who He is—inside our hearts so we would manifest that glory to the world.

> He put His glory—everything that makes God who He is—inside our hearts so we would manifest that glory to the world.

We have to let go of the old notion of "Jesus in our heart" and realize that the glory of God, the glory of the Ancient of Days, is shining *in us* and desires to shine *through us*. As Paul wrote:

> *But we have this treasure in earthen vessels, so that the surpassing greatness of the power will be of God and not from ourselves; (2 Corinthians 4:7, NASB).*

Paul understood there was something greater than himself on the inside of him. This greatness was a treasure, hidden in a vessel of clay, waiting to be revealed to the world. He later writes:

> *To them [you and me] God has chosen to make known among the Gentiles the glorious riches of this mystery, which is Christ in you, the hope of glory (Colossians 1:27, NIV).*

He also wrote:

> *Don't you realize that all of you together are the temple of God and that the Spirit of God lives in you? (1 Corinthians 3:16, NLT).*

The God of the universe, the King of Ages lives inside of you. In the same way the Ark of the Covenant was once the abiding place of God's glory, you and I are now His consecrated containers, set apart for Him. If people want to experience His divine glory, they must encounter His earthly vessels, you and me. We are God's house.

> If people want to experience His divine glory,
> they must encounter His earthly vessels,
> you and me. *We* are God's house.

Moreover, Jesus is the light, the glory that shines in and through us to a dark and dying world. So how does this light shine through us? Through our gifts. Jesus said:

> *"You are the light of the world. A city set on a hill cannot be hidden; nor does* anyone *light a lamp and put it under a basket, but on the lampstand, and it gives light to all who are in the house. Let your light shine before men in such a way that they may see your good works, and glorify your Father who is in heaven"* (Matthew 5:14–16, NASB).

Don't hide your gifts under a bowl of insecurity, ignorance, or neglect. Let them shine so the world can see Jesus for who He really is. Glorify God. Show the world *who* God is in His fullness as you use your gifts. Remember, God has given everyone something to do that shows who He is (1 Corinthians 12:7). That *something* is the gift within you, and what you *show* is the glory of God.

What will be the result when we do that? *Yada*—a revelation of God's glory. In addition, that will inevitably lead to the world "glorifying our Father who is in heaven." Sounds like a revival.

18

The Mirror

If God's glory is the only all-satisfying reality in the universe, then to try to do good for people, without aiming to show them the glory of God and ignite in them a delight in God, would be like treating fever with cold packs when you have penicillin.

—*John Piper*

When you exercise your gifts, you display God's glory. But why? Why does God want to be glorified? Is He an egotist or a braggart with a never-ending thirst for attention? I'm going to attempt to answer this with two answers.

Remember, we will be the most satisfied when God is glorified through us.

First, God wants to display His glory because He loves us so much. He wants to give us what can truly satisfy us and make us eternally happy. John Piper explains this concept:

> God is the one being for whom self-exaltation is the most
> loving act, because he is exalting for us what alone can satisfy
> us fully and forever. If we exalt ourselves, we are not loving,
> because we distract people from the one Person who can
> make them happy forever— God. But if God exalts himself,
> he draws attention to the one Person who can make us happy
> forever— himself. He is not an egomaniac. He is an infinitely

glorious, all-satisfying God, offering us everlasting and supreme joy in himself. (Piper, 2013, 725–729).

We must realize that His desire to be glorified and our fulfillment are not mutually exclusive. Our desire for an exciting, fun-filled, and satisfying life isn't contrary or at odds with His glorification. They are one and the same, if we do it according to His plan and design. Remember, God is glorified when you are satisfied, truly satisfied.

> We must realize that His desire to be glorified and our fulfillment are not mutually exclusive.

Second, the reason God desires to reveal His glory has to do with *change*. Change is the byproduct when we behold God's glory. Change is the purpose of the journey. It is ultimately God's will for our lives. He wants us to display the image of Christ in us, but before He can, something has to change. Moreover, that something is *us*. One of my favorite life verses explains the relationship between the glory of God and the transformation He desires for us:

> *But we all, with unveiled face, beholding as in a mirror the glory of the Lord, are being transformed into the same image from glory to glory, just as by the Spirit of the Lord*
> *(2 Corinthians 3:18, NKJV).*

According to this verse, part of God's master plan to fulfill the prophecy of Habakkuk 2:14 is to redeem and transform us—the purpose of His glory is change. Even more, whenever God reveals His glory, the opportunity for change exists.

So, can we glimpse the glory of God *now?* We can—which brings us back to our dreams, our calling, and our gifts. Let me take you back to an earlier time in my life. Do you remember the story of my encounter with God's Spirit at the beginning of the book? That day God opened my eyes to a divine dream. I loved music, even as I was busy going to school. I was honing my skills as a musician and singer when I could. At the time, I felt prompted by the Holy Spirit to spend thirty minutes in prayer each night. Therefore, each night, usually late, I would go out to my family's sun porch and pray. I'd walk back and forth, laboring in long prayers and . . . I felt nothing. No manifestations of anything. No holy lights. No voices from heaven. Just sore feet and a tired voice.

Then, after several weeks, I suddenly felt the presence of God on the sun porch one summer night. I don't know how to describe it. I just *knew* God was there. This was a big event for a Presbyterian teenager. I didn't hear a piano playing softly or a preacher telling me the presence of the Lord was with me, I just knew He was there. The atmosphere grew thicker and thicker, and for no reason I could identify, tears began flowing down my face. What could I do? I began pouring out praise to God, telling Him what He meant to me, and thanking Him.

Then, in the middle of all that praise, I felt Him tell me to be quiet. Maybe He has never worked with you that way, but it was just what I needed at that moment. I needed to be quiet and listen. God wanted to tell me something. He wanted to *show* me something. I felt that it was time to be silent before God.

In addition, there, in His invisible presence, He showed me something. Do you want to know what I saw? God showed me His glory! Don't think I'm super spiritual. I didn't see the train of God's robe filling up His throne room, as Isaiah did. I didn't see a river flowing out of the heavenly temple of God. I didn't see a blinding light come down in the room out of the vast expanse of space and sky with a roll of thunder.

No. None of that.

Instead, I saw . . . get ready . . . *myself.*

That's right. *Me.*

Now you're probably thinking, "This guy must be totally into himself!" The truth is, that's what I saw. And it was burned into my spiritual eyes even to this day. I didn't see myself as I was then, a nineteen-year-old college student. I saw myself in the future. I saw myself standing up and playing a keyboard with a microphone in front of me. I could see thousands and thousands of people with their hands lifted to the Lord. I was singing and leading them in worship. Moreover, in that vision—in that *dream*—I knew I was singing a song that I had written.

In an instant, I saw and comprehended all of this. A picture is really worth a thousand words because I could use a thousand words to describe what I saw in that one millisecond. More accurately, I saw *God's view and opinion of me*—His true, perfect, and complete view and opinion of me.

From my perspective, it was a *future me*. From God's eternal, all-knowing perspective, it was the *real me* yet to be discovered. The *real me* hidden from natural eyes. The *real me* who for nineteen years had been looking in the wrong mirror reflecting the views I had of myself, the views my loving parents had of me, and the views the god (little "g") of this world had. It was a distorted view, a filtered view. There was a *real me* waiting to step forward, rise up, and explode on God's stage for the world to see.

For years, I've told this story repeatedly as I've described the glory of God. I know the vision I saw that day was instrumental in changing me. In the years since that experience, I've had many such "glimpses" of God's glory. Some were as memorable as that one, and some were much less dramatic. Nevertheless, *all* of them have had the same effect on me—they led me to change. And until recently, I never quite understood why.

I recently had the privilege to speak at a conference attended by pastors and worship leaders from across the country. A friend, Sam Maxwell, was also one of the guest speakers. During one of his sessions, he described the glory of God much as I had been describing it for years. God's glory manifests who He is. It's His nature and character revealed to us. It's everything that makes God . . .

God. Then Sam explained another dimension of God's glory that I had overlooked. He began to describe the *doxa* of God and how it affects those of us who are in Christ (Maxwell, 2014).

So, the glory of God is actually God's view and opinion of us!

Sam directed our attention to something I had read many times before but had never really seen. The word *doxa* means "the opinion, the judgment, the view, and the estimate of worth, the value of someone" (Spicq and Ernest, 1994, 1:362). This definition can help us understand what we mean when we say, "the glory of God." Look at my life-verse again with this definition inserted:

> But we all, with unveiled face, beholding as in a mirror the [view and opinion] of the Lord, are being transformed into the same image [His view and opinion of us] from doxa to doxa, just as by the Spirit of the Lord (2 Corinthians 3:18, Paraphrase).

That is why we behold "as in a mirror." It's as if we're looking at ourselves, except with *His* perspective, with *His* view, and with *His* opinion. So, the glory of God is actually God's view and opinion of us! That's what I saw that night on the sun porch. I saw God's *view and opinion* of Sion Alford. I saw His glory as if I was looking in a mirror.

I didn't see the face of Jesus or the *Shekinah*, but I looked in a prophetic mirror and saw myself as *God saw me*. I saw an image of me transformed more into the likeness of His Son. I saw myself using my gifts to glorify God, and I saw myself utterly satisfied in Him. I caught a glimpse of a dream fulfilled. In addition, when I saw His glory, *the change* began.

Every morning when I wake up, I face the reality of another mirror. This one, however, is conveniently located in our bathroom.

It covers nearly the entire span of the sixteen-foot wall above our vanity. It would be difficult to overlook it. I use it every morning, every evening, and at other times during the day. It's very useful. For what? For reflecting me!

Isn't that why we look into mirrors? We want to see ourselves. When we wake up in the morning and prepare ourselves for the day, why do we stop by the mirror in our bathrooms and look in the mirror? We do that in case we need to *see something needs to change.* Mirrors are tools for fixing and checking things. Mirrors help us know what to change, comb, paint, tuck, or brush. Mirrors help us see things that we wouldn't otherwise see. Have you ever tried to fix your hair without a mirror? Mixed results, right? It doesn't work very well.

> Mirrors show us how others perceive us. Mirrors change our perspective. They allow us to see our blind spots. They reveal *truth.*

Mirrors show us how others perceive us. Mirrors change our perspective. They allow us to see our blind spots. They reveal *truth.* As much as I hate it sometimes, they don't lie. Mirrors tell the truth. Mirrors always tell the truth. And God's mirror does the same thing, but with a slight twist. When we gaze into His mirror, it reveals something more common to all of us—it shows us where we need to change on the *inside.* Just like that mirror in my bathroom, I use God's mirror to help me correct and adjust according to the things I see. When I look into God's mirror, I see His glory—His *view and opinion* of me. In addition, God's mirror supernaturally reveals where I need to change by showing me who I can be if I allow the Holy Spirit to transform me.

The image of the mirror also appears in the book of James:

> *Do not merely listen to the word, and so deceive yourselves.*
> *Do what it says. Anyone who listens to the word but does*

not do what it says is like someone who looks at his face in a mirror and, after looking at himself, goes away and immediately forgets what he looks like. But whoever looks intently into the perfect law that gives freedom, and continues in it—not forgetting what they have heard, but doing it—they will be blessed in what they do (James 1:22–25, NIV).

God's Word serves as another manifestation of the glory mirror. When we look into that mirror of truth, we see ourselves the way God sees us. We see where we need to change, what needs to change, and we alter the perspective we have of ourselves. Anyone who listens to God's Word—who looks into the mirror of truth and does what it says, will fix what needs to be fixed, repair what needs to be repaired, or correct whatever problem may exist. Then God will bless us in the things we do. Sounds like a good promise, correct? The mirror of His Word shows us where we need to change, because that is what truth does.

> The mirror of His Word shows us where we need to change, because that is what truth does.

Truth reveals our weaknesses, not to belittle or devalue us, but to show us how much we need God's grace. Remember, the greater the dream, the greater the vision. And the greater the vision, the more we have to change. Why is this so? Because the reason why a dream is a dream is that it helps us see ourselves different than we are today. Something has to change and that something is us.

So step in front of the mirror and behold His glory—God's view and opinion of you!

19

It's Time to Change

Everyone thinks of changing the world, but no one thinks of changing himself.

—*Leo Tolstoy*

What makes a dream a dream? Why was the vision of seeing myself singing and playing the piano a dream? The answer is simple. I couldn't do what I had seen in my dream at that very moment. In fact, I didn't even know how to play a piano or a guitar at the time. Even more, even if I did have the ability, I wasn't positioned with a platform to sing and play in front of that many people. Sure, I had sung before, but certainly not a song that I'd personally written. Moreover, I definitely had not sung in front of more than fifty people.

The dream was bigger than I was.

That's the power of a dream—it shows us that we need to *change*. In addition, the bigger the dream, the more change we need in order for it to happen. This idea seems very simple, but it's an important one to understand if we want to fulfill God's call and purpose in our lives.

What makes our dreams seem big and inspiring is their distance from reality. When God first revealed His dream for me, I was singing in a small church to a crowd of about thirty people with a cassette tape as my accompaniment. Even so, my future would be singing and playing the piano with excellent musicians in front of thousands of people in venues larger than any arena I had ever seen at the age of nineteen.

What needed to change?

At first, you might think the same thing that I did—I needed to learn to play a piano and find a bigger venue to perform. But that is not what I needed. In fact, that's a major reason I wrote this book. God doesn't give us dreams to inspire us to have more ambition and greater action; He gives us dreams to inspire us to *change*.

> God doesn't give us dreams to inspire us to have more ambition and greater action; He gives us dreams to inspire us to *change*.

God shows us a dream to awaken us to the changes we need to make in ourselves. Our first reflex, however, is often to try to change our surroundings and environment to look like the picture we see in our dream. If you do this, you'll eventually become frustrated and disappointed because you can't control your surroundings or environment. If you try to change those things without first changing yourself, you'll only end up discouraged. You will be unprepared for the dream. In fact, the dream may actually destroy you.

In his dream, Joseph projected himself into the future. However, in his immaturity, he decided to push the dream along and try to change his surroundings by sharing his dream with his brothers. He may have thought they too would embrace his dream and quit picking on him so much. I don't really know. However, I *do* know that Joseph's dream demanded change. Nevertheless, that change had to happen *in* Joseph, before it could happen *through* Joseph. It wasn't Joseph's environment that needed a transformation; it was Joseph's character. *He* needed to change.

Moses needed to change. Paul needed to change. David needed to change. Gideon. Joshua. Abraham. Samuel. James. John. The list goes on and on. Every individual God called and gave a glimpse into the glorious future had to embrace the true purpose of the dream—*change*. Our dream requires change and transformation in order for it to become a reality in a healthy way.

> Our dream requires change and transformation in order for it to become a reality in a healthy way.

Look again at Paul's words. This verse reveals the relationship between God's glory, His view and opinion of us, and the transformation that results from encountering Him:

And we all, who with unveiled faces contemplate the Lord's glory, are being transformed into his image with ever-increasing glory, which comes from the Lord, who is the Spirit (2 Corinthians 3:18, NIV).

The word Paul used for "transformed" here is *metamorphoo*, which means, "to change the essential form or nature of something—to become, to change, to be changed into, to be transformed" (Louw and Nida, 1996). Paul used the same word in Romans 12:

Do not conform to the pattern of this world, but be transformed by the renewing of your mind. Then you will be able to test and approve what God's will is—his good, pleasing and perfect will (Romans 12:2, NIV).

On that summer night, when I beheld the glory of the Lord "as in a mirror," I saw myself in the future, and I didn't look like I did in the present. I saw myself as God saw me. Change needed to happen. I needed a renewed mind, and the dream I saw became my inspiration to submit myself to the Lord's process. I didn't know it at the time, but my vision that night would encourage me through the dark, lonely nights ahead.

What is your dream? Have you seen yourself in the future? Do you have a correct view and opinion of yourself? You might be thinking, "No, I don't have a dream. I don't know my purpose." If those are your thoughts, I'm actually going to take a risk and disagree with you.

Why do I disagree? Because I am certain that God has given you moments to behold your glorious future "as in a mirror." You have seen. Maybe you haven't recognized those moments yet, because they weren't as dramatic as the one I described, but you *have* had them. So with that in mind, here's a simple test: If you can answer "yes" to any of these three questions, then God really has given you a dream and a purpose:

1. Does a problem or conflict in life irritate you because you can see the solution to the problem? It is so clear and easy to understand. This problem could be in your family, society, industry, work, or even the government—if so, that is part of your dream.
2. When you see people doing things that you know God called them to do, does something deep inside of you jump? Are you stirred? Can you see yourself doing that or something like that? If so, that is part of your dream.
3. Have you been through a major crisis in your life? Did that crisis give you a special compassion for people who may be going through something similar? Do you instinctively want to help them? There it is again—if so, that is part of your dream.

I could continue with other questions, but these three will pertain to most of us. However, I need to make a very important disclaimer that goes along with these questions. Just because you answered "yes" to one of the questions doesn't mean your purpose will look exactly like the fulfillment of God's purpose in someone else's life.

Shortly after my encounter with God, I went to a concert to see my favorite Christian rock band, Mylon LeFevre and Broken Heart. Seeing Mylon and his band on the stage made my insides jump! What they did was awesome and the glory of God was pouring out from their ministry and gifts. I thought to myself, "I *must* be called to do the same; why else would I feel so passionate about something?" I thought God had called me to the contemporary Christian music scene to share the gospel like these great pioneers of contemporary Christian music. My heart was pure, but my perception was off. Their calling was similar to mine, but mine was very different. God's plan for me was unique.

Be careful with taking God's dream for you and trying to work things out in your own mind. You can mislead yourself. Operating on your own sends you down a painful path of disappointment and heartache; just ask Joseph. Remember, the purpose of God's dream for you is *change*, and that change is about what's happening *in* you, not *around* you.

Remember, the purpose of God's dream
for you is *change*, and that change is about
what's happening *in* you, not *around* you.

The reason why God wants to be glorified is to redeem the world. Moreover, that redemption starts with the beholder—with you. When God reveals His glory as in a mirror, true revival will begin. Divine detours are designed. So look at yourself in God's mirror.

20

King of the Hill

The weight of His glory, exalted in worshiping the Father and magnifying His Son in the power of the Holy Spirit, impacts, reshapes, and alters our character and conduct. It liberates, releases, and loosens us from the hold of sin and self and unleashes the ministry-life of Jesus Christ to course through our daily lives.

—Jack Hayford

I once heard the saying, "Everybody wants change . . . until it happens." Most people want to fulfill their dreams and do great things, but few want to change in order for that to occur. Most of us prefer for everyone else and everything around us to change instead. We feel like our circumstances and situations have to change before we can fulfill God's call on our lives.

Change is uncomfortable, and most of the time, it costs us something. In the case of transforming into the image of ourselves reflected in the mirror of God's Word and the glory we behold, that sacrifice we make is the sacrifice of *self.* Jesus understood this fact. Many who followed Him over Judea's dusty hills wanted to "follow" Jesus, but few wanted to experience the change that is required to walk genuinely with Him:

> *Then Jesus said to his disciples, "If any of you wants to be my follower, you must turn from your selfish ways, take up your cross, and follow me" (Matthew 16:24, NLT).*

This edict from Jesus applies to us as well. If we want to follow Him, we must understand and obey this simple, three-part requirement for walking in His steps.

The first step in following Jesus is to "turn from our selfish ways" or, as another translation says, we "must deny ourselves." As fallen humans, we have a sickness. We are *selfish*, and we live in a world that revolves around *self*. Jesus understood this, so He began His decree by saying that if you want to follow Him, truly follow Him, you begin by denying the innate selfish mentality embedded in every human heart. Every human heart has a throne. Moreover, it is *always* occupied. Even more, someone is in charge of appointing who or what sits on your throne—and that someone is *you*.

As a kid, one of my favorite games to play was "king of the hill." I'm sure almost every child has played it at some time—at least until someone got hurt! Among my friends, the game always started whenever a dump truck deposited a large load of dirt somewhere in our neighborhood. Sometimes it was at a construction site, other times they placed a pile where they needed fill dirt. The rules of the game are simple. Whoever can stay the top of the hill is "king." If someone else can climb up and knock off the "king," then that person is the new "king of the hill." It's a great game, especially for the "king." It's not quite as much fun if you are the person who the "king" is always knocking down the hill, which happened quite often in my case. If you were a smaller kid, you made being "king" fun—especially for the "king." I was usually one of the people who made it fun as I went rolling down the hill with sand in my mouth and pants.

However, in our hearts, we also have a "king of the hill." Sometimes big "bullies" occupy a space in our hearts. They smash, bash, and trash anything that tries to knock them off the top. How did they get there? Unlike the childhood game, these kings don't climb and conquer. We *place* them there. They are appointed by the only person who can place them on the throne of your heart—*you*.

God designed and built us with this throne inside us—the throne of our hearts. Whatever is on the throne is the center of our worship. Whoever is on this throne is glorified. Whatever is on this throne is worshipped. And this is a painful truth: If something or someone other than God occupies this place in our hearts, then we have become idol worshippers, and whatever's on the throne of our hearts has the ability to *change* us.

> If something or someone other than God occupies this place in our hearts, then we have become idol worshippers, and whatever's on the throne of our hearts has the ability to *change* us.

We learned how the glory of God—seeing an image of God and His view of us—has the power to change us. The flipside of that is true as well—it is possible to exchange the glory of God for the glory of something else. Look at what Paul wrote to the Romans:

> *For although they knew God, they neither glorified him as God nor gave thanks to him, but their thinking became futile and their foolish hearts were darkened. Although they claimed to be wise, they became fools and exchanged the glory of the immortal God for images made to look like mortal human being and birds and animals and reptiles (Romans 1:21–23, NIV).*

Then in verse 25, Paul says:

They exchanged the truth about God for a lie, and worshiped and served created things rather than the Creator—who is forever praised. Amen (Romans 1:25, NIV).

When we exchange the glory of God for the glory of *any* other image, we enter the area of idolatry; we become idol worshippers. You might object: "Hey, I don't have any wooden statues in my house that I bow down to every night." When God refers to idolatry, He's not limiting the discussion to golden statues and wooden images.

So what exactly is an idol? An idol is *anyone or anything* that takes the place of God in your life. Whatever has your affection, your attention, and your heart more than God is an idol. If God does not sit on the throne of your heart, then an idol does. Idolatry is nothing more than misplaced worship, misdirected love, and misaligned affection. Myles Munroe said, "Whenever we worship idols, we prostrate both our glory *and the glory of God within us* before unworthy things" (Munroe, 2005, 53). Wow! When we don't let God take His rightful place on the throne of our hearts, we exchange *His* glory—the glory inherent within us—for the far inferior glory of an idol.

Isn't that exactly what the Israelites did?

At Horeb they made a calf
and worshiped an idol cast from metal.
They exchanged their glorious God
for an image of a bull, which eats grass (Psalm 106:19–20, NIV).

What a slap in God's face! When we bend our knees at the altar of an image, it is a disgrace. It goes against our created nature put there by God. We worship something that is lower than God and ourselves. It violates our Creator. Think of it as God saying, "You are created in *my* image, you are the carrier of *my* image, and I do not bow my knee to anyone or anything."

So why do we do this? Why do we bow down to lesser gods? Because we are "worship beings," and we can't help it. God created us to worship. Something has to be "king of the hill." Someone has to be king. *This* is why idolatry is so prevalent. It's why the first two of the Ten Commandments are as follows:

> *"You shall have no other gods before me."*
> *"You shall not make for yourself an image in the form of anything in heaven above or on the earth beneath or in the waters below. You shall not bow down to them or worship them; for I, the Lord your God, am a jealous God . . ."* *(Exodus 20:3–5, NIV).*

When Adam and Eve first sinned against God, idolatry fueled this desire. They exchanged the glory they already had—the greatest glory possible—for the false promise of a greater glory. They traded in their God for a lesser god. What a tragedy. Matt Papa describes this problem: "We have taken the diamond of God's glory to the pawn shop of the world and traded it for a penny. A diamond for a picture of a diamond" (Papa, 2014, 66). Yes, we traded an ocean for an aquarium and a majestic snowy mountain range for a tourist-trap souvenir postcard bearing the image of a mountain. Why did we do this? Because we believed a lie. Eve believed a lie. Adam believed a lie. Moreover, you and I have believed the same lie. We thought it would *satisfy*.

> *"Eve," said the serpent, "Surely God is holding back something real glorious. He knows there's something more than Himself and He doesn't want you to experience it because it would make Him unnecessary. It will satisfy your curiosity and the hunger that you have"* *(Genesis 3:4–5, paraphrased).*

Isn't that ironic? Satan laced his words to Eve with just enough truth to sound good and just enough lie to kill. That's still his standard mode of operation today. Adam and Eve traded the truth of God for a lie. They gave up their glory for the glory of created things. They exchanged what alone could satisfy their hunger for something that would leave them always wanting more. Never again would they be satisfied in this world.

> When we replace our satisfaction with Him
> with something else, we will never be satisfied.

Isn't that the purpose of glory? It satisfies an innate hunger in each person. Remember, we are only satisfied when He is glorified. When we replace our satisfaction with Him with something else, we will never be satisfied. Still, we think something will satisfy us more or cost us less. There it is—cost . . . us . . . less.

Do you want to walk the walk of worship? Do you want to take the divine ordained detour? Do you want to go from promise given to promise fulfilled? That journey is filled with opportunities to get rid of your idols and replace them with something that can truly satisfy—*Him*. However, it *will* cost. There is a price to pay for following Him on the road of His will. Moreover, while it's not always easy, it *is simple:* "If any of you wants to be my follower, you must turn from your selfish ways, take up your cross, and follow me."

21

Ready to Change

*It may be hard for an egg to turn into a bird: it would be a
jolly sight harder for it to learn to fly while remaining an egg.
We are like eggs at present. And you cannot go on indefi-
nitely being just an ordinary, decent egg. We must be hatched
or go bad.*

—C. S. Lewis

In the last chapter, we established that whatever you place on the
throne of your heart is also the center of your worship. Even
more, did you know that whatever you worship is also what you
become? Whatever you worship *changes* you. In addition, it changes
you into its image.

How does this happen? It's because we sacrifice to it. As mentioned earlier, sacrifice is necessary to follow Jesus. If you're going
to walk in the will of God on the road to His promise, sacrifice is
necessary. Moreover, sacrifice always leads to change:

*Therefore, I urge you, brothers and sisters, in view of God's
mercy, to offer your bodies as a living sacrifice, holy and
pleasing to God—this is your true and proper worship. Do
not conform to the pattern of this world, but be transformed by
the renewing of your mind. Then you will be able to test and*

approve what God's will is—his good, pleasing and perfect will (Romans 12:1–2, NIV).

When we offer our lives, our flesh, and our bodies as a living sacrifice to Him, we are transformed by the renewing of our minds. When we worship, change is inevitable. Moreover, since we are always worshiping, we are always changing.

> Whatever has your affection and your attention,
> will change you to become more like it.
> We will conform to *its glory*—its opinion of us.

This truth is another reason idolatry is so harmful. Whatever has your affection and your attention, will change you to become more like it. We will conform to *its glory*—its opinion of us. Whatever we let occupy the throne of our hearts will dictate how we change:

> *The idols of the nations are silver and gold,*
>   *made by human hands.*
> *They have mouths, but cannot speak,*
>   *eyes, but cannot see.*
> *They have ears, but cannot hear,*
>   *nor is there breath in their mouths.*
> *Those who make them will be like them,*
>   *and so will all who trust in them (Psalm 135:15–18, NIV).*

Notice that this Psalm doesn't say that only those who make idols will be like them. It also says *those who trust in them* will be like the idols. Whether you make the idol yourself or simply trust in them to satisfy you, they will change you. You will become a reflection of the thing you worship. Does this experience sound familiar? What you behold, you also become. What you worship, you become. Whatever has your eyes has your future.

When I saw God's glory that evening on that sun porch in Florida, I began a long process of change. I saw *His* opinion, *His* estimate, and *His* view of me and I began to change into that person by the power of the Holy Spirit.

What you behold, you also become.
What you worship, you become.
Whatever has your eyes has your future.

But not long after, I began to "exchange" God's glory for another glory—one less costly and one I thought could get me to the promise faster. Before that night, I had other idols—my fishing boat, my ATV, and my hunting gear. Those were not bad things but, for me, they were misaligned things. I also had an idol that so many people have faced—*the desire for success*. I wanted to succeed and make money. I chose the field of pharmacy to feed that desire. Pharmacists make a lot of money. There's nothing wrong with that, unless it's the motivation sitting on the throne of your heart and occupying a place only God should have.

So what did I do? Tear those idols down and throw them away? Did I pile them in a big pile and burn them? No, I replaced them with another idol. That is what we often do with idols. We don't really remove them; we only replace them. Just like the bully on top of the hill, you can't politely ask him to step down. You have to climb up there, knock him off, and replace him. Idols are not removed; *idols are replaced*.

I replaced my idols of fishing and hunting with playing the piano and singing. I replaced my idol of wanting success and money with the idols of ministry greatness and fame. These were "better" idols, or so I thought at the time, because God was behind them.

I saw the picture. I beheld the glory, right? All that was left was getting from here to there.

God showed me a picture of myself in the future to encourage me to go through the necessary change to get there. I traded God's glory for a shortcut, an idol that I created through my own efforts. Many people try to do that, and it certainly came natural to me. As a result, I started to worship idols that looked more "Christian" instead of Christ Himself. Wow. That hurt just saying it. Nevertheless, it is true. I let the "good" replace "God."

Sadly, many people believe this kind of theology today:

"Give your heart to God and He'll make sure you'll always be rich."
"Pursue your dreams."
"Sacrifice for your goals today to achieve your destiny."

That is what I did. I honestly thought I was putting God first, but I really wasn't. Deep down, I was pursuing a dream instead of the God of that dream.

I had replaced my childish idols with more adult ones. And I changed into a monster. I became selfish. I became self-seeking and self-promoting. I climbed ladders while stepping on people to get there. I was becoming like my idols. Moreover, because my idols were a mess, I became a mess.

So when that happens, how do you turn it around? How can it genuinely change? Simple—behold a greater glory. In 2 Corinthians 3, the apostle Paul wrote about how Moses' face shone with God's glory when he descended the mountain of God. Simply being in God's presence transformed Moses' appearance so much that he had to wear a veil over his face to lessen the intensity of the glory shining from it. He wore the veil until the glory faded (Exodus 34:31–32). Paul spoke about the afterglow of glory:

The old way, with laws etched in stone, led to death, though it began with such glory that the people of Israel could not bear to look at Moses' face. For his face shone with the glory of God, even though the brightness was already fading away. Shouldn't we expect far greater glory under the new way, now that the Holy Spirit is giving life? (2 Corinthians 3:7–8, NLT).

What is the new way? Paul continues:

If the old way, which brings condemnation, was glorious, how much more glorious is the new way, which makes us right with God! In fact, that first glory was not glorious at all compared with the overwhelming glory of the new way. So if the old way, which has been replaced, was glorious, how much more glorious is the new, which remains forever! (2 Corinthians 3: 9–11, NLT).

Paul is writing about an overwhelming glory, one that lasts forever and never fades—a *greater* glory. It never fades—leaving us empty and dry. It perfectly satisfies.

This principle is simple: The only way to remove a lesser glory is to replace it with a greater glory. That is how we change.

The only way to remove a lesser glory is to replace it with a greater glory.

When we exchange lesser glories, like fame and fortune, with the greater glory of God Himself, something marvelous happens:

But whenever someone turns to the Lord, the veil is taken away. For the Lord is the Spirit, and wherever the Spirit of the Lord is, there is freedom (2 Corinthians 3:16–17, NLT).

Freedom! Yes, true freedom from sin's influence and grasp. Freedom to live right. Freedom to do what is right. It is not a religious freedom with a stifling load of rules and regulations, but a freedom that actually frees. That kind of true freedom leads to true change:

> *So all of us who have had that veil removed can see and reflect the glory of the Lord. And the Lord—who is the Spirit—makes us more and more like him as we are changed into his glorious image (2 Corinthians 3:18, NLT).*

In verse 16, Paul wrote about "whenever someone turns to the Lord." *That* is true repentance. Turning away. Changing direction. Changing the things at which we look. Changing our focus. He has our attention. He captivates our gaze. As we behold Him, and we see Him for who He is. We see His *doxa*—His opinion, His view, and His assessment of us. That's how we change. That's how transformation begins. From *doxa* to *doxa*. From glory to glory.

> *Beloved, now we are children of God; and it has not yet been revealed what we shall be, but we know that when He is revealed, we shall be like Him, for we shall see Him as He is. And everyone who has this hope in Him purifies himself, just as He is pure (1 John 3:2–3, NKJV).*

I now have this hope. That is why I don't do the things I shouldn't. And that hope is in Him, the One who drives me away from sin and into His arms.

22

Be Holy

*If I know my own heart today, I would rather die than live as
I once did, a mere nominal Christian, and not used by God in
building up His kingdom. It seems a poor empty life to live for
the sake of self. Let us seek to be useful. Let us seek to be vessels
meet for the Master's use, that God, the Holy Spirit, may shine
fully through us.*

—Dwight L. Moody

Why is it so important to walk as Jesus walked? Why is it
necessary to pursue holiness when God has already given
you gifts and talents? Isn't it enough that you want to serve Him
and let your gifts show His power and glory? Isn't God going to be
God, no matter how righteous you are? Why does He require you
to be like Jesus?

These are great questions. I've asked them myself. I've seen both
extremes—those who are one breath away from hell and those who
are one breath away from heaven, because they have so much of the
character of Christ. God uses each type of person to display His
glory. Each of them demonstrates God's grace on earth. However,
holiness and purity are vital for participating in His grand display
of glory on the earth. Why is this? David's journey to return the
Ark of the Covenant back to its rightful place in Jerusalem gives a

great picture of God's divine plan for those who want to be carriers of His glory:

> David and all Israel went to Baalah of Judah (Kiriath Jearim) to bring up from there the ark of God the Lord, who is enthroned between the cherubim—the ark that is called by the Name.
> They moved the ark of God from Abinadab's house on a new cart, with Uzzah and Ahio guiding it. David and all the Israelites were celebrating with all their might before God, with songs and with harps, lyres, timbrels, cymbals and trumpets.
> When they came to the threshing floor of Kidon, Uzzah reached out his hand to steady the ark, because the oxen stumbled. The Lord's anger burned against Uzzah, and he struck him down because he had put his hand on the ark. So he died there before God (1 Chronicles 13:6–10, NIV).

These verses tell a strange and disturbing story. King David wanted to restore the Ark of the Covenant to its rightful place with God's people. The Israelites had left it years before in the house of Abinadab. David's motives appear to be pure. He arranged magnificent worship to accompany the Ark, and he joined in celebrating its homecoming. But he wasn't a priest, nor did he respect the ways God prescribed for transporting the Ark. Apparently, the priests in charge of moving Israel's most sacred symbol of God's presence didn't know much more than David.

Several years before, the Philistines had stolen the Ark and held it captive in the temple of Dagon, a Philistine deity. When the Philistine citizens suffered a mysterious disease outbreak and then found their idol facedown before the Ark, they decided to send it back, saying, "The ark of the God of Israel must not remain with us, for His hand is severe on us and on Dagon our god" (1 Samuel 5:7, NLT). So, they loaded the Ark on a "new cart" pulled by two cows "on which there has never been a yoke," a gesture of honor based on their own pagan traditions. They also sent guilt offerings in the same way they would give highest reverence to their gods. They did the best they knew to do, because they didn't have God's Word or any history with the Lord, so He spared them from further punishment. God's show of mercy reminds me of a verse we looked at earlier:

"... And I will be gracious to whom I will be gracious, and will show mercy on whom I will show mercy" (Exodus 33:19, ESV).

God could have just as easily killed the Philistines, but He didn't. They experienced His hand of mercy, and He delayed their time of judgment. David, Uzzah, and the priests, however, *should* have known better. They were without excuse. When they transported the Ark on a cart drawn by oxen, following the example of the Philistines rather than God's commandments, it ended in disaster. The men transporting the Ark treated it only slightly better than a trunk of clothes. And as it rattled along, it began to tip over. Uzzah put out a hand to steady it. That gesture resulted in his immediate death. That seems terribly harsh, doesn't it?

Uzzah probably felt responsible, intending to keep the Ark from crashing into the dust. Unfortunately, he and the other men failed to comprehend the seriousness of their job. They treated the symbol of God's special Covenant as something common. And Uzzah died because David and the priest handled the Ark in a way that reflected their attitude toward God. They treated the Ark of the Covenant like a piece of furniture instead of a holy vessel of God's glory, because they didn't understand the nature of the God of the Ark—and of all the people, the king and priests should have known.

They treated the Ark of the
Covenant like a piece of furniture
instead of a holy vessel of God's glory.

Somewhere between chapters 13 and 15 of 1 Chronicles, David
and the priest did their homework. They researched and found that
God had prescribed a specific way to carry the Ark. Now informed,
David told the priest: "It was because you, the Levites, did not
bring it up the first time that the LORD our God broke out in anger
against us. We did not inquire of him about how to do it in the
prescribed way" (1 Chronicles 15:13 NIV).

As a pharmacist, I know a little bit about prescriptions. I particularly like the way David said this. He said there was a "prescribed
way" to carry the glory of God. Deviate from the "prescribed way"
and suffer the consequences. When I worked as a pharmacist, I
would fill over 250 prescriptions a day. If I worked a 5-day week,
that came to about 1,250 prescriptions. If I worked 45 weeks in a
year, that would be around 56,250 prescriptions. Do you know how
many errors the state of Florida legally allows a pharmacist to make
in one year?

Zero.

Make one mistake in those 56,250 prescriptions and I could be
sued and even imprisoned if someone was harmed. Is that scary?
Have you ever tried to read the handwriting from a sixty-year-old
physician who didn't write much better when he was twenty-five?
It's not easy, let me tell you. Nevertheless, I wasn't allowed any
excuses. I had to get it right *every single time*. I had to fill the prescriptions in "the prescribed way" that I learned during six years of
pharmacy school—no mistakes allowed.

The state of Florida would not allow me to forget the precepts
I had learned while in pharmacy school, and David shouldn't have
forgotten God's laws either. God's tolerance was zero when it came

to handling the Ark. His glory wasn't something for the Israelites to take lightly.

The second time, though, with the priests consecrated for service, David fulfilled a lifelong dream to deliver the Ark of God to a place that was prepared, sanctified, and consecrated for it. Consecration isn't a word most people know. I know it sounds very holy, but we should understand it if we're going to be conduits and effective administrators of God's glory. The word means, "to set apart as sacred, to observe as holy, to dedicate" (Strong, 2001). Consecration, sanctification, and holiness are necessary if we want to associate ourselves with the glory of God. It is not a suggestion God makes; it is a life or death decision that we make. Touch His glory with unclean hands . . . die.

Good motives don't justify bad actions.

Just ask Uzzah. He had good motives, I'm sure. However, good motives don't justify bad actions. God held Uzzah accountable for knowing His commandment, which clearly stated:

> *"After Aaron and his sons have finished covering the holy furnishings and all the holy articles, and when the camp is ready to move, only then are the Kohathites to come and do the carrying. But they must not touch the holy things or they will die . . ." (Numbers 4:15, NIV).*

Understand that this isn't only an Old Testament commandment. God also demands those of us on this side of the cross to be holy and separate if we desire to be a vessel of His glory:

> *Now in a great house there are not only vessels of gold and silver but also of wood and clay, some for honorable use, some*

for dishonorable. Therefore, if anyone cleanses himself from what is dishonorable, he will be a vessel for honorable use, set apart as holy, useful to the master of the house, ready for every good work (2 Timothy 2:20–21, ESV).

The great house Paul mentioned here is the kingdom of God. The vessels to which he refers are you and I. If we want God to use us for the honorable things of His kingdom, then we must cleanse ourselves from anything that is dishonorable. Then He will set us apart as holy, consecrated, prepared, and dedicated for every good work. This sounds like a great promise. Even so, remember, consecration is up to us.

The process of consecration is also called sanctification. God makes us holy by the process. Sanctification is God's will. Paul tells us that God wills for us to be sanctified:

For this is the will of God, that you should be consecrated (separated and set apart for pure and holy living): that you should abstain and shrink from all sexual vice,

That each one of you should know how to possess (control, manage) his own body in consecration (purity, separated from things profane) and honor (1 Thessalonians 4:3–4, Amplified Bible, Classic Edition).

God wants us to be sanctified. Through the process of sanctification, we will know how to manage our bodies in a way that is holy and honorable. That is God's will. He wants us holy because He is holy:

But just as he who called you is holy, so be holy in all you do; for it is written: "Be holy, because I am holy" (1 Peter 1:15–16, NIV).

David and the priest figured out this principle. They realized that in order to transport the glory of God from one place to another, the vessels carrying God's glory had to be consecrated. They learned His glory cannot be shouldered with human innovation, rather with human consecration. The burden of revealing God's glory to the world must rest upon consecrated shoulders. We can't accomplish this by human strength, power, or devices. The responsibility to honor the glory of God rests with those whose hearts have been given over to God completely and whose character has been prepared by Him through the process of sanctification.

They learned His glory cannot be
shouldered with human innovation,
rather with human consecration.

23

Christlike Character

Once we realize that the Father's goal is not just to save us but to transform us, we will continually find that God has one answer to all our spiritual problems: appropriate the nature of His Son!
—Frances Frangipane

Consecration doesn't exactly sound like a lot of fun. We don't really like to talk about it. It involves many heavy terms like separation, holiness, sanctification, and purity. Someone who wants to carry the glory of God to the world must take on those qualities of character. Nevertheless, what does that mean in our day-to-day lives? How am I consecrated? How do I cultivate the kind of character God wants in His servants? Moreover, what exactly is "character" anyway?

I've heard a few good definitions. Character is being true to your reputation. Character is doing what's right when no one is looking. Character is saying what you mean and meaning what you say. Those are all true, but character is more than what you think of yourself or what others perceive about you. According to God, whose standard is ultimately definitive, character is the extent to which we are like Christ.

When I say "like Christ," I don't mean that you have to become someone other than yourself. To be "like Christ" is to have the same kind of relationship with the Father that the Son did while He was on earth. He continues to have that kind of relationship now. The more we become like Christ, the more we become who God created us to be. True humanity, for the first humans, included perfection. However, they sinned. Because of their sin, all humans became less human. Sin separated us from God and, therefore, we became less than who God meant for us to be. To become like Christ is to become more like the person God designed and created you to be, to become more authentically "you." More like the image you have seen in the *glory mirror*. More like the *doxa*.

When we trust in Christ for salvation, He begins a work within us to transform us into His likeness. Through this progressive renovation and transformation of our character, we gradually become the people God envisioned us to be when He created us. We take on the view, the estimate, and the opinion God has of us—the *doxa*. As this happens, our gifts are revealed and they become "useful to the Master and prepared to do any good work" (2 Timothy 2:21, NIV), resulting in glory shown together and glory revealed.

Now, let's put all of these things together—Christlike character, the glory of God, and our gifts. How do they all relate? God calls us to be consecrated, set apart for His special use, to be Christlike, so that we *desire* to use His gifts to reveal His life-changing glory. I want to revisit Paul's message to Timothy. Look at how it relates to character and why it is so important:

> *In a large house there are articles not only of gold and silver, but also of wood and clay; some are for special purposes and some for common use. Those who cleanse themselves from the latter will be instruments for special purposes, made holy, useful to the Master and prepared to do any good work*
> *(2 Timothy 2:20–21, NIV).*

Godly character is necessary if we want to be instruments useful to God. The more we cleanse ourselves from dishonorable things, the more useful we become to the Master. *God appreciates talent, but He promotes character.*

God appreciates talent, but He promotes character.

The world does not work this way. We witness the opposite constantly in politics, sports, and business; the talented are promoted without regard to their character. The world promotes talent and hopes the character will be there, but often it is not. And what happens? Their gifts take them places their character can't hold them.

Turn on sports news and you'll see this displayed—another star athlete found outside of a bar or some place he shouldn't be. I recently saw a story about a pro athlete who was shot in a bar. I remember thinking, "That man makes six million dollars a year! That's about thirty thousand dollars for each play he makes in a game! Why would he waste his time in a place like that?" Clearly, he was there because his talent took him too far, too fast, and his character couldn't keep up.

The same kind of thing happens in politics; many voters tend to overlook weak character when it comes to elections. That's why we're never very surprised when a dynamic and charismatic individual wins the election, only to be caught later, having an affair, stealing tax dollars for personal expenses, or casting a vote in exchange for a bribe.

Sadly, we can't really look down on athletes and politicians, because this way of thinking has also infiltrated the church. I'm sure you've seen it. A congregation and its leaders promote someone on the merit of talent to hold a position that their character can't sustain. Often, just due to the nature of the calling, Christian leaders attract the most attention when they fall. We might see a talented speaker or a gifted musician. The church can't wait to get them on a platform, but they can't handle the attention that comes with holding that microphone because they don't have a solid foundation of character.

Many times, I receive phone calls from other worship pastors saying, "My pastor wants me to promote someone, but if I do, this person is going to cause so much trouble. Their voice is outstanding, everyone gets goose bumps, but they lack character, and it is a disaster waiting to happen."

This type of catastrophe is a significant problem in the church because the people who stand in front of the congregation are like the priests who carry the Ark. They must be consecrated to bear the glory of God before others. Without the benefit of strong, Christlike character, they will inevitably fall, and the consequences can be devastating for everyone. Let's be honest, no one is shocked when a politician turns out to be a philanderer; it's not as if our expectations were that high. On the other hand, when a spiritual leader like a pastor, a worship leader, a teacher, or a counselor fails morally, the ripple effect of sin affects so many more people. Sadly, the world really takes notice because they, sometimes more than people in the church, place extremely high expectations on God's public representatives. They know what God has called us to do, and they take devilish delight in finding fault because they're looking for an excuse to deny God.

That's another reason I felt compelled to write this book. That's the reason potential worship leaders at my congregation, Gateway Church, commit to spend from nine to twelve months waiting and training before they ever stand on the platform in a worship service. That's also the reason why Paul tells believers to be transformed by the renewing of their minds as one aspect of their worship (Romans 12:1–2). It takes a conscious choice to think and operate contrary to the world, because our old nature defaults to sinful, selfish ways of thinking.

God may have you given a magnificent gift of cooking, uncommon abilities as a salesman, the singing voice of an angel, or the ability to hold audiences transfixed by your speech. Regardless of your gift, someone will receive glory. Who will it be? Your character will determine who is glorified. As mentioned earlier, your gifts come with a responsibility of service; it's your character that determines who is served.

> Your character will determine who is glorified ... your gifts come with a responsibility of service; it's your character that determines who is served.

Understand that while the character of God's vessels is paramount, especially with those who lead others, God doesn't expect perfection. He has called us to be holy, not perfect. However, He does expect progress. He wants to see us being changed into that image that we see in the mirror of His Word, from glory to glory, from *doxa* to *doxa*. If we needed perfection before we could minister His grace, all of our churches would be empty and no one's testimony would be heard. No one would qualify to display His glory until the King of Glory returns. He is the only one who is truly perfect.

He flows through holy vessels, not perfect vessels.

So, Christlikeness is a process, not a destination. It's a process that involves denying yourself, taking up your cross, and following Him. It's a walk. It's a journey.

It is on this divine detour that we will develop more and more of His character in our hearts, until others have noticed just as they did with the early disciples:

When they saw the courage of Peter and John and realized that they were unschooled, ordinary men, they were astonished and they took note that these men had been with Jesus (Acts 4:13, NIV).

24

Inside Out

Conduct is what we do; character is what we are. In the economy
of grace, conduct is the offspring of character. Character is the
state of the heart, conduct its outward expression.
—E. M. Bounds

Soon after my experience with God that summer night, I
became fervent in my pursuit of the dream. My motives were
right (at least I thought they were) and I wanted nothing more
than to fulfill everything God had for me. I wanted to fulfill His
call on my life. I wanted to make a difference in the world. What
I didn't realize was that what *He* wanted and what *I* wanted were
two different things. I wanted the dream to happen, and He wanted
me to be transformed, renewed, and changed into the person I saw
in the dream. I wanted a platform. God wanted a process. I wanted
comfort. God wanted character.

I wanted a platform. God wanted a process.
I wanted comfort. God wanted character.

During those early years in my walk with God, I thought I
could get character the way many Christians think you should:

Go to Bible school, pray more, read the Bible more, fast more, and yes, be the first one to go down to the altar every time the pastor or a youth group speaker says, "If you want more of God, get down here." However, here's what I have learned since then. You can't get more character at a church altar. You can't get more character through the laying on of hands or having someone pray for you. Character is not imparted; character is earned. Character is not to be received; Character has to be refined.

> Character is not imparted; character is earned. Character is not to be received; Character has to be refined.

I'll even go a step further and say you can't get more character by reading your Bible, praying, or fasting. Before you throw this book across the room and yell, "Heresy!" let me explain. Those things may facilitate God's work in your life to bring about more character, but doing those things will not *guarantee* that you will have more character. Simply doing those things doesn't make you more like Him.

Our *response* to what we read in God's Word is what brings about change. Our *response* to what we hear in prayer is what brings about change. Our *response* to what we gain in fasting is what brings about change. If you think otherwise, you're as deceived as the Pharisees were. They thought reading the Scriptures, praying, and fasting made them holy. They worked extremely hard to look like the image they read about in the Torah, but their hearts were corrupt and sinful. They prayed loud and long public prayers, but they never obeyed the One to whom they were praying. They fasted more than anyone did, yet their appetites for self-gain were never satisfied. Why? Because their motives were based on earthly glory, not heavenly glory. They wanted to impress people more than God:

"And when you pray, do not be like the hypocrites, for they love to pray standing in the synagogues and on the street corners to be seen by others. Truly I tell you, they have received their reward in full . . ." (Matthew 6:5, NIV).

When we try to get more of God or more character through our religious activities, we end up like these Pharisees. Our focus is on conforming our outward appearance to look holy, instead of allowing Him to transform us from the inside out. Jesus described what happens when our motivation is driven by external appearances:

"Woe to you, teachers of the law and Pharisees, you hypocrites! You clean the outside of the cup and dish, but inside they are full of greed and self-indulgence. Blind Pharisee! First clean the inside of the cup and dish, and then the outside also will be clean" (Matthew 23:25–26, NIV).

So how does God develop His character inside of us? The apostle Paul said that God has promised to transform us by the Holy Spirit from within. In fact, God's Word promises that He will complete what He started despite our own inconsistencies and failures:

And I am convinced and sure of this very thing, that He Who began a good work in you will continue until the day of Jesus Christ [right up to the time of His return], developing [that good work] and perfecting and bringing it to full completion in you (Philippians 1:6, Amplified Bible, Classic Edition).

Notice that the change happens *within* you. Sure, the outside will begin to change at some point during this process, but the change comes from the inside out:

May God himself, the God of peace, sanctify you through and through. May your whole spirit, soul and body be kept blameless at the coming of our Lord Jesus Christ. The one who calls you is faithful, and he will do it (1 Thessalonians 5:23–24, NIV).

He called us, and He *will* be faithful to complete His work in us. So what is our part? Submit to the process. Embrace the plan of God. Yield to His purpose. Take the divine detour. *That* is how character is developed. That's how God transforms us into His image from glory to glory. God didn't just call you and then hope you work out all the details at some point in the future. No, He has a plan and He is faithful to do it.

God doesn't want an empty shell who can sing. He doesn't want to use people who will glorify themselves or exalt their gifts. He wants authentic worshippers. He doesn't want your gift; He wants *you*.

In truth, the church doesn't need your abilities; it needs *you*. God doesn't need your gifts; He wants *you*.

If we forget that truth, our character will begin to slide. We will begin to value others and ourselves in terms of abilities rather than who we are as individuals and as members of Christ's body. We will forget that people have inherent worth because we each represent uniquely crafted works of divine art. We bear God's image. In truth, the church doesn't need your abilities; it needs *you*. God doesn't need your gifts; He wants *you*.

25

The Path to the Promise

When God gives a promise, he always tries our faith. Just as the roots of trees take firmer hold when they are contending with the wind; so faith takes firmer hold when it struggles with adverse appearances.

—Robert Murray McCheyne

The journey towards our divine destiny isn't easy. Detours are never convenient. Sometimes life is a like a fire in which we are refined and prepared for the purposes and callings of God. When we come to terms with the fact that our dreams and gifts aren't all about us, then we begin to see God's all-consuming, grand purpose for our lives. The ultimate and highest calling of all believers is to represent the likeness of Jesus on the earth through our surrender, humility, and desire for unity. Christlikeness is simply talking like, walking like, and looking like Jesus. When we are Christlike, we accurately represent Him. He is seen, His glory is beheld, and God is glorified.

As a lead worshipper, I join fifteen people on a platform and lead thousands in worship during Gateway Church's weekend services. All the lights and cameras are pointed at us. The platform in our building is elevated, so we physically stand above those we lead. Whether or not I like it, people look at our team differently; they remember our faces when they see us at the movie theatre or in a restaurant. In addition, because they know our faces and positions, they take notice of how we treat our servers, how we conduct ourselves under pressure, and how we deal with temptation. It's not fair, but people hold spiritual leaders to a higher standard. Because of this "occupational hazard" of spiritual leadership, I tell people plainly, "If you don't like it, get off the platform! The privilege of serving God comes with the burden of responsibility."

When we combine all of this with what we discussed about dreams, promises and purposes, we arrive at another significant conclusion: *If you get to the promise, to the dream, without cultivating Christlike character, the promise will destroy you.*

If you get to the promise, to the dream, without cultivating Christlike character, the promise will destroy you.

Remember, God gives us dreams for two reasons: First, to show us where we need to change, and second, to give us hope for the future. Joseph could endure his difficult prison years because he knew God wouldn't fail to keep His promise. By the end of his ordeal, Joseph learned he didn't need to pursue what God had already promised; he only needed to focus on doing God's will day-by-day, moment-by-moment. Knowledge of his dream helped him make wise decisions when choices came his way, but he learned to remain quietly in the moment as he answered the question, "What would God have me do right here, right now?"

This statement may shock you, but I hope it will shake the misperceptions you may have about the will of God. The will of God is *not* the promise of God (Gorman, 2004). That's right, the will of God and the promise of God are not the same thing. The promise of God is something that *inspires*. The will of God is something that we *do*. God calls us to *do* His will, not His promise. You can't *do* a promise!

Let me say it another way: the promise of God for your life is not God's will for your life.

The promise of God for your life is not God's will for your life.

So why does God give a promise? He gives it to inspire us to do His will, to endure hardship with patience, to receive blessings with gratitude, to enjoy success with wisdom, to face fear with confidence, and to follow His leading when it seems to carry us away from what *we* consider the fulfillment of the dream. This walk requires faith, because sometimes the will of God appears contrary to the promise of God. Let me say it this way: Sometimes the will of God doesn't look like the promise of God. Even more, sometimes the will of God looks like it is taking us in the opposite direction of the promise of God!

I discovered this truth at nineteen years old, when I caught a glimpse of God's promise for me and felt a strong urge to begin the chase. While my heart wanted to run headlong after my dream, I somehow knew God wanted me to continue with my pharmacy degree program. Today, when I tell people my story, they often give me a look that says, "If you knew you were called to a ministry of music, songwriting, and worship leading, why did you waste time on a pharmacy degree?" I simply shrug and explain that God knew what He was doing. I didn't. So I decided to trust Him.

Let me illustrate this principle another way. Most people can tell by my accent that I was reared in the South. Actually, I'm from

LA—Lower Alabama. Though I was born in Alabama, I grew up in a region of Florida just below the Alabama border. Today, I live in a suburban neighborhood where no one mows his own lawn. In 1970s Alabama, we cut our own grass. Saturday mornings, my dad would wake me up and tell me to get up and mow.

"Alright! Get up! Let's go outside and work till we sweat and throw up!" he'd say with a sense of humor only dads have.

I'd say, "Dad, how long's this going to take?"

"We work 'til it's done, even if we die tryin'!"

Death by sweat. I can't say I was very motivated. So, when I became a dad, I decided to handle things a little differently. I learned from my own dad's negative motivational model (which did work, by the way), and I gained wisdom from God's positive example. Now, when I want to motivate my sons to mow the grass, I take a slightly different approach. I wake them up on Saturday morning and I say, "Alright boys, today we're going to the batting cages and hit some baseballs! After that we're going to Dairy Queen and have us some Blizzards!" I haven't even finished my sentence before the boys are jumping on their beds singing my praises.

Then, I say the words all parents have said one million times to their children: "But first . . . ."

"But first, we've got to mow the lawn."

My promise is the batting cages and a chocolate Blizzard. My will is that we mow the yard. My promise and my will are two different things, yet they are related to each other in a special way. We can see this principle as the author of Hebrews writes:

You need to persevere so that when you have done the will of God, you will receive what he has promised (Hebrews 10:36, NIV).

The promise is the reward for doing the will of God; the will is for doing and the promise is for inspiration.

The will is for doing and
the promise is for inspiration.

Do the promise; miss the will. Do the will; receive the promise. The pattern I've seen in the Word of God is this: God always tells us the promise before He reveals His will to us. If He showed us His will first, many of us wouldn't take the first step of the journey. Sometime I wish God had a "but first" conversation with us before He released us into the world to fulfill our calling, but He doesn't —at least not in the same conversation when He tells us His promise. I believe that He doesn't tell us immediately, because it would scare many of us away from taking that first step in the journey.

If we went back in time to visit King David when he was a boy, we might tell him, "Listen David, you're going to be the King of Israel. But first, you're going to have to endure rejection, have a couple spears thrown at you, and hide among the caves in the desert for a while." God anointed David as king of Israel *long* before God fulfilled the promise.

We could also have a conversation with a teenage Joseph: "Someday, you'll become Prime Minister of the greatest civilization in the world. Your family and most of the other people in the world will bow before your authority. *But first,* you're going have to suffer the betrayal of your brothers, find yourself sold into slavery, be falsely accused of attempted rape, and languish in prison for a few years, during which time everyone you know will have mourned you as dead."

Thankfully, God doesn't show us everything in His initial conversations with us concerning His promise. Otherwise, who would have the courage to obey? Like many people, I'm glad I didn't know where the path to my promise would take me, or I would have never started the divine detour. "Hey, Moses, you're going to be the deliverer of My people from slavery, but first, My will is that you spend forty years on the backside of a desert tending sheep." Would anybody sign up for that? Not many.

By His grace, God works much differently. First, he shows us His promise and *then* He reveals His will as we take each new step. The divine detour He ordains becomes the way to fulfill the promise in the right way, at the right time, so our character grows into the dream.

26

Obscurity

*Character cannot be developed in ease and quiet. Only through
experience of trial and suffering can the soul be strengthened,
ambition inspired, and success achieved.*

—*Helen Keller*

While I walked the divine detour God had for me—being
called to a ministry in music, yet obediently earning my
pharmacy degree—I didn't have it all together. By God's grace, He
kept my feet on the path of His will despite my many attempts to
take shortcuts to the dream. Today, I can't fully explain what God
had in mind or why He took me on such a roundabout route. Even
so, I count myself blessed by the process. I wasn't born with the
greatest talent. If so, I might have succeeded in taking the fast track
to my dream, but I wouldn't have had the character to hold me once
I arrived. I had to work hard in a field where no one applauds a job
well done.

I had to spend some time in *obscurity*. Where did David go
right after the prophet Samuel anointed him? Did he get himself
fitted for a new crown? No, he went back to the backside of a
dusty desert to watch his father's sheep. That was hardly a promotion. In fact, that pasture outside of Bethlehem looked just as
it did before his anointing—boring and hot. He didn't jump on

social media to post about the prophetic words just spoken to him by one of the greatest prophets of Israel. He didn't look for attention or ask for a special place of privilege. Instead, he went about doing his father's business just as he had faithfully done before his anointing. He stayed in the will of God. Luke writes:

"And when he [God] had removed him [Saul], he raised up David to be their king, of whom he testified and said, 'I have found in David the son of Jesse a man after my heart, who will do all my will'" (Acts 13:22, ESV).

Did you catch that? David had a heart after God. The object of David's pursuit wasn't his dream. It was God, the Dream Giver. He was after God's heart, and the proof of that desire was His desire to do God's will.

During my tenure with obscurity, on the backside of a desert called pharmacy school, God began His work on my need for approval. In my own perspective, I was totally overlooked and underappreciated. I can't count the number of times I tried to take a shortcut past God's character development program. But every single time, He brought me back to His will. Trust me, it wasn't pretty. But about three years into pharmacy school, I found myself sitting in the parking lot of a hospital in Gainesville, Florida, wearing a lab coat and stethoscope, bawling my eyes out. I sat in the car listening to some worship music, crying out, "Why, God? What am I doing here? You called me to worship ministry. You called me to be a psalmist and a songwriter. So, what am I doing here? Where am I going?"

That hospital parking lot didn't look like the dream I'd seen years earlier. More than that, I felt even further away from it! This was my prison in Egypt (Genesis 39), my wilderness in Midian (Exodus 2), and my cave in Adullam (1 Samuel 22). If I'd had the right perspective, I might have understood that I *was* in the center of God's will, even though it seemed completely wrong. I would have known I was traveling the path God had mapped out *for my good*. That knowledge just might have saved me from a lot of heartache and pain, because it would have kept me from trying to take shortcuts.

If you have a dream and you're wondering why your circumstances don't look anything like your promise from God, take comfort, you are most likely right in the center of God's perfect will! "But it hurts and I don't like it!" you may be saying. That may be true. There are no shortcuts to the promises of God. There is only obedience to His will. In addition, when it comes to obedience, it's not a question of whether we're going to suffer in this journey; it's a question of deciding how we will suffer.

> There are no shortcuts to the promises of God. There is only obedience to His will.

No one likes pain, but as followers of Jesus, we must understand that true biblical suffering is necessary, and we must learn to embrace it. Why? First, when we suffer righteously, we share Christ's experience on earth, which allows us to know Him more deeply:

> *. . . that I may know him and the power of his resurrection, and may share his sufferings, becoming like him in his death (Philippians 3:10, ESV).*

Everybody wants to be like Jesus until they realize that the cup of Christlikeness is a bitter cup. It will cost. There will be some pain involved, and that pain happens as we crucify self.

Second, when we suffer well, our pain becomes someone else's comfort. Paul reassured the Corinthian believers:

Praise be to the God and Father of our Lord Jesus Christ,
the Father of compassion and the God of all comfort, who
comforts us in all our troubles, so that we can comfort those
in any trouble with the comfort we ourselves receive from God
(2 Corinthians 1:3–4, NIV).

Nothing qualifies you to minister to the needs of others like your limp. We discussed earlier that what you go through could make you either *bitter or better*. Choosing better means that you'll be able to minister to those who are suffering, especially those suffering through similar circumstances that you once endured.

Third, suffering can produce two positive byproducts: character and hope. Character is most often harvested in the field of suffering. Remember, we don't get character from God through an act of instant impartation. It comes because of walking through suffering. Paul outlined this formula for character development when he stated, "Not only so, but we also rejoice in our sufferings, because we know that suffering produces perseverance; perseverance, character; and character, hope" (Romans 5:3–4, NIV). Character and hope are the byproducts that occur when we mix suffering and perseverance together.

I want to clarify something at this point. I want to clear up any misunderstanding about suffering in the kingdom of God. Suffering for Jesus has been wrongly associated with things such as cancer, tragic events, and the like. I don't believe this is the type of suffering God called us to endure. These things happen and God can work for good in such events, but the true biblical suffering to which Paul refers is different. Godly suffering involves one key critical ingredient—a heart willing to do the will of God no matter the consequences. If you do the will of God, you will suffer. That is biblical suffering. The other things I mentioned are a result of a fallen world caused by human sin. However, the biblical suffering that leads to character and hope is caused by our obedience to God's will.

Does all of this seem like good news? You probably aren't praying, "God, I want more of You, I want to be more like Jesus. Please lead me through painful trials and tribulations so I may suffer!" If you're anything like me, you're probably not praying that prayer.

27

Are We There Yet?

*Patience is not simply the ability to wait—it's how we behave
while we are waiting.*

—*Joyce Meyer*

When my wife and I lived in Florida, we would take our children to Disney World every February. The trip took about six hours, and for the three energetic kids we had at that time, that felt like a lifetime. Very early in the trip, we would hear their squeaky voices from the back seat of our minivan. Every fifteen minutes like clockwork, they would ask, "Are we there yet?" We've all heard it before, right?

Patience might be a virtue, but it isn't found in great quantities in a four-year-old. It doesn't come naturally; none of us were born with it. It is something that we must develop. Sometimes people say, "I'm not a very patient person. It's not in my personality." I have some news: Patience isn't a part of *anyone's* personality. All of us have a deficiency in vitamin P (patience) regardless of our personalities.

Patience is the starting block of character.

How important is patience? Patience is the starting block of character. It's the ingredient found in every recipe for Christlikeness. Patience is the first step we all take to develop the godly character:

> Not only so, but we also glory in our sufferings, because we know that suffering produces perseverance; perseverance, character; and character, hope. And hope does not put us to shame, because God's love has been poured out into our hearts through the Holy Spirit, who has been given to us (Romans 5:3–5, NIV).

Suffering produces perseverance or as some translations say, *patience*. I don't really like the word perseverance. Just the sound of it concerns me. The heart of the word is "severe." However, the Greek term here means "to bear under," like an Olympic weight-lifter who is determined to hold a massive barbell over his head until the signal sounds to drop it. He really perseveres—"bears under" or "endures"—until the trial has passed. It's neither comfortable nor painless, but if we want character, we must embrace it as a friend and not run from it like a disease.

In those three verses in Romans, we see that the first product of biblical, God-allowed suffering is patience. Ambrose Bierce said, "Patience is a minor form of despair, disguised as a virtue." It never comes easy. It usually doesn't begin in us until we are irritated. Until we are irritated with our present situation or circumstance, we don't have to call upon patience. If we're not irritated or our flesh isn't screaming, we are not exerting patience, we're merely *waiting*.

Waiting occurs when timeliness isn't important to us. Many times, I've sat on our fifteen-passenger van and waited in the driveway for everyone to load up so we wouldn't be late for church. We now have eight kids, and it's not always possible to get every one of them motivated to be on time. With one eye on my watch and the other on the garage door, I internally calculate the speed we need to drive in order to get to our destination on time. With each passing minute, the required speed increases proportionally. However, there is always a point when my waiting enters *the patience zone*. Calculations don't matter at that point. My mind is too blurred to calculate speed any longer. All that matters is we must leave and we must leave *now*!

Patience didn't start in me until I reached the point of irritation. I was no longer in charge of the timing of the journey. Someone else was given those reins. I usually reach that place where I want to rest my hand on the horn and *HONK* until I motivate the stragglers. I am done waiting! Now I must be patient despite the time. Patience enters the room when the clock matters.

Isn't that what patience is all about? Time? "Are we there yet?" Isn't that also what our divine detour is all about? Time? We hear the call, see the vision, get the prophecy, and we're ready to fulfill the dream! But *wait*. Better yet—have *patience*. The journey is about time. But it is not our timing; it is *His* timing. Character isn't made in a microwave; character is made in a crock-pot. It is slow cooking, and God controls the temperature.

> Character isn't made in a microwave; character is made in a crock-pot. It is slow cooking, and God controls the temperature.

For this reason, patience is important for the development of our character. This is why patience is the first byproduct of suffering. Patience begins when we realize that we're not in control, especially when it comes to the timing and duration of the situations and circumstances in which we find ourselves. When we exercise the patience that suffering produces, we stay on the road of His perfect will. F. B. Meyer wrote:

> Think it not strange, child of God, concerning the fiery trial that tries thee, as though some strange thing had happened. Rejoice! For it is a sure sign that thou art on the right track. If in an unknown country, I am informed that I must pass through a valley where the sun is hidden, or over a stony bit of road, to reach my abiding place—when I come to it, each moment of shadow or jolt of the carriage tells me that I am on the right road. So when a child of God passes through affliction he is not surprised (Meyer, 1917, 9).

Patience is proof that we have surrendered our hearts to God's will. Impatience is evidence that *self* remains in charge, alive and well. A yielded heart is patient because it knows God is doing His perfect work. He is in charge and self is not. James wrote:

> *But let* patience *have its perfect work, that you may be perfect and complete, lacking nothing (James 1:4, NKJV, emphasis added).*

Patience is proof that we have surrendered our hearts to God's will. Impatience is evidence that *self* remains in charge, alive and well.

Patience has a *perfect work*—character, and its goal is to make you perfect and complete. It is the thermostat by which God controls the atmosphere of your heart.

During our annual family trek from Panama City to Orlando, we must have heard "are we there yet?" three hundred times. However, something else also happened during the journey. The kids got anxious and quickly upset each other. That's no surprise. By the time we reached the halfway point of our trip, two were fighting over a toy from McDonalds, one was complaining that someone was touching him, and another was throwing French fries. They had lost perspective. Somewhere along the journey, they forgot something—they forgot they were going to DISNEY WORLD! They cared more about the temporary discomfort of cohabiting a minivan than they did about the amazing place they were going to visit. They wanted their current situation and circumstances to change immediately instead of recognizing that their temporary discomfort was for a purpose—to get them to the promise!

Therefore, I did what all fathers do in situations like that. I calmly interrupted their childish tirades and said, "Dearest children, please refrain from the provocative attitudes of disruption and protestations of injustice and remain composed and collected until we reach our final destination." Ha! Not really! My response was more like this: "Give me that toy so I can throw it out the window! Then we'll see who will fight over it!" In all seriousness, I actually acted the way I think God does in many of our uncomfortable situations—I reminded them of the promise. I told them the journey was going to be worth the pain. Be patient. We will get there. Enjoy the trip.

They were willing to trade Disney World for an Indian River Fruit Stand on Interstate 75, because they had lost perspective. That's what happens to us so often when we're on the road of God's will. Sometimes we lose perspective and want to trade the promise of God for something of far less value. However, when this urge to trade away our promise arises, that is precisely the time we should embrace the way of suffering so that patience can have its way in us.

Suffering may have a byproduct, but so does patience— character. Jesus lived this way. He experienced this. The author of Hebrews wrote about it:

. . . Keep your eyes on Jesus, who both began and finished this race we're in. Study how he did it. Because he never lost sight of where he was headed—that exhilarating finish in and with God—he could put up with anything along the way: Cross, shame, whatever. And now he's there, in the place of honor, right alongside God. When you find yourselves flagging in your faith, go over that story again, item by item, that long litany of hostility he plowed through. That will shoot adrenaline into your souls! (Hebrews 12:1–3, *The Message*).

Jesus has led the way for us. He plowed through the suffering. We *will* get there. The journey will be over one day, so maybe we should quit asking, "Are we there yet?" And maybe we should start asking, "God, am I done yet?"

28

Surprised?

Patience has its perfect work in the school of delay.
                                                    —*E. M. Bounds*

So what are we supposed to do while we're in the place where we have to exercise patience? The apostle Peter gives the answer:

Dear friends, do not be surprised at the fiery ordeal that has come on you to test you, as though something strange were happening to you. But rejoice inasmuch as you participate in the sufferings of Christ, so that you may be overjoyed when his glory is revealed (1 Peter 4:12–13, NIV).

Remember, sometimes walking in God's will looks nothing like His promise. Our situations and circumstances look strange to us because we don't expect them. We expect everything to go the right way because we love God and want to do His will. Then an unexpected event occurs, and we immediately respond with bewilderment: "Where did that come from?" or "Why did God let this happen?"

In times like these, what is God's word to us? Don't be surprised. Nothing strange is happening. Meditate on this for a few minutes: Nothing comes into your life unless God allows it. Let it sink in. Nothing. Not . . . one . . . thing. *Nothing* happens unless God allows it. This is hard medicine for us to take, especially if we've been through tragic situations. I know that I have.

> Nothing comes into your life unless
> God allows it. Let it sink in.
> Nothing. Not . . . one . . . thing.

Several years ago, my wife and I had the opportunity to take in our five additional children, our nephew and nieces. They had just lost both their mother and father to tragic diseases. These orphaned kids needed a home where they could stay together as a family, and we were the designated beneficiaries. Do you wonder if I questioned how God could allow such a tragedy to befall these innocent, young children? You bet I did. During the initial days with funerals and visits to the lawyers, Shannon and I certainly doubted God and questioned if His will was good. Nevertheless, during those times we clung to this familiar verse:

And we know that all things work together for good to those who love God, to those who are the called according to His *purpose (Romans 8:28, NKJV).*

We clutched that verse during this great ordeal. Our whole family did. God allowed it for a reason. I'm not saying He caused it, but He did allow it. Today, many years later, I can see that good has come out of it. Sure, I would much rather have Michael and Stacy here to live life with us, but I do see the good it has done in our hearts and the hearts of our eight children. Because of what we went through, I feel that I've become more like Jesus. He developed His character in me during the time of suffering we endured. Not only in me, but also in the hearts of Shannon, our three natural children, and our five adopted children. We are better today, not bitter, because of what we experienced.

However, simply going through something doesn't make you a better person. Going through trials and tribulations doesn't actually create character in you. If that were true, we might all glow in the dark! No, going through things doesn't change you, but *how* you go through things determines if you will change. I know many people, who've been through much worse situations, but they're not better people; they're bitter people. It's not *what* you go through that develops character; it's *how* you go through it that develops character. God has given all of us a choice to walk in His will toward His promise. Will we allow our circumstances to harden our hearts or change us? The author of Hebrews writes:

So, as the Holy Spirit says:

"*Today, if you hear his voice,*
 do not harden your hearts
as you did in the rebellion,
  during the time of testing in the wilderness" (*Hebrews*
  3:7–8, NIV).

During times of testing, our hearts can be hardened if we rebel, if we jump off the road of His will, or if we do not let patience have its work in us. Remember, nothing comes into our lives unless God allows it.

It's not *what* you go through that develops character; it's *how* you go through it that develops character.

"*Why* did God allow it?" is not a helpful question. Instead, our question should be "*What* does He want to do in me as I walk through this?" God's goal is not our comfort; His goal is our Christlikeness. Paul writes to the Romans:

> *And we know that all things work together for good to those who love God, to those who are the called according to His purpose. For whom He foreknew, He also predestined to be conformed to the image of His Son, that He might be the firstborn among many brethren (Romans 8:28–29, NKJV).*

He "foreknew," or as I might say, "He knew beforehand" that you and I are called and destined to be conformed into the image of His Son. All things work together to make this happen. All things. The good, the bad, and the ugly things. It all works together to make us into the image of His Son.

> God's goal is not our comfort;
> His goal is our Christlikeness.

Max Lucado recently spoke at our church. During his sermon, he shared an illustration that described this verse in Romans in a way I will never forget. He had a small table on the platform and on top of it was a coffee maker, some water, a coffee pot, coffee filters, a coffee cup, and some ground coffee. Then he said:

> If I were to take any of these individual components of this system of coffee making and try to enjoy it, it would not be very rewarding. A coffee filter, by itself, is useless and unpalatable. The wires that plug into the wall, the cup, and the coffee pot are not enjoyed individually. Even the ground coffee itself is quite harsh and bitter. But

something special happens when *all of these things work together*. A wonderful aroma emanates. A warm, rich flavor is released. The result of things coming together is a savory sip of delicious coffee. Why? Because *all things worked together for good!*

Many times, our present trials seem like a dry coffee filter or an empty coffee mug when, in reality, those things were allowed because God is brewing something better. He is bringing many things together to create a masterful blend. He is allowing things into our lives so we can become more like Christ. God foreknew this about each of us. This is our purpose; this is our destiny.

What are we to do when life presents us with an unknown ingredient? The apostle Peter told us how to act:

> *But rejoice inasmuch as you participate in the sufferings of Christ, so that you may be overjoyed when his glory is revealed (1 Peter 4:13, NIV).*

Rejoice! That is what we are supposed to do! Don't complain—praise! Don't grumble—be grateful! As Paul said:

> *Not only so, but we also rejoice in our sufferings, because we know that suffering produces perseverance; (Romans 5:3, NIV).*

I love this verse in Romans because it shows me that God doesn't ask us to praise Him *for* our suffering; we are to praise God *in* our suffering. No right-minded person is thankful *for* pain *while* it's happening, but we can all be thankful *in* our pain. When we do this, when we praise God during the storm, our perspective remains secure. God enables us to see the big picture and realize that He is making something beautiful out of the mess.

Remember, the pain has a purpose.
The process has a goal. Our job is
to rejoice. His job is to refine.

Remember, the pain has a purpose. The process has a goal. Our job is to rejoice. His job is to refine. There is a desired result, an end purpose to it all:

> In all this you greatly rejoice, though now for a little while you may have had to suffer grief in all kinds of trials. These have come so that the proven genuineness of your faith—of greater worth than gold, which perishes even though refined by fire—may result in praise, glory and honor when Jesus Christ is revealed (1 Peter 1:6–7, NIV).

The purpose for the pain is simple. It reveals Jesus Christ. Because when it happens, people see the glory of God. They see Him as He is. They gain a genuine revelation of who He is. The less they see of you, the more they see of Him. You and I are the vessels carrying that light burden. Don't be surprised when trials and problems come. He knows you are ready for them. He knows you can handle it. He knows exactly what's over the next hill, and it is *much* better than Disney World!

29

The Multiplier

Suffering isn't an obstacle to being used by God. It's an opportunity to be used like never before.

—*Levi Lusko*

We've discovered that suffering produces patience and patience produces character. But exactly *how* does this happen? How does waiting until patience kicks in create character in us? Sure, we may get to the point where we're irritated and want God to synchronize to our timing, but what does that teach us? The answer is simple, but it must not be underappreciated: *Obedience.*

We can summarize the entirety of our relationship with God in this one word. Our obedience is the evidence of our relationship with Him. It is the leading indicator of a real, genuine relationship between God and us. When the Pharisees asked Jesus to name the greatest commandment, He answered:

. . . *"Love the Lord your God with all your heart and with all your soul and with all your mind"* (*Matthew 22:37, NIV*).

Jesus knew the answer, because He had passed the test. He knew His love and devotion for the Father could be found in the fruit of His obedience. He knew we couldn't love God and not obey God. Those two things go hand-in-hand:

> *And this is love: that we walk in obedience to his commands.*
> *As you have heard from the beginning, his command is that you*
> *walk in love (2 John 6, NIV).*
>
>   *If you keep my commands, you will remain in my love, just*
> *as I have kept my Father's commands and remain in his love. I*
> *have told you this so that my joy may be in you and that your joy*
> *may be complete (John 15:10–11, NIV).*
>
>   *"If you love me, keep my commands" (John 14:15, NIV).*

You can't love God without obeying Him. It simply isn't possible.

So what does love have to do with suffering? Everything. Remember the verse we spoke of in the previous chapter:

> *And we know that all things work together for good to those who*
> *love God, to those who are the called according to His purpose.*
> *(Romans 8:28, NKJV).*

All things do not work together for the good of *everyone*. The verse above tells us that all things work together for the good of those *who love God* and who are *called according to His purpose*. Two conditions: love and calling.

There are many that go through difficult things and it does not work out well. Their situations do not end in "good." Why? Because they didn't love God through the trial and they lost sight of the His purpose. Let me explain why.

As we've learned, suffering produces patience, and patience produces character. Right now, my pharmacy-educated brain is begging to give an example, so indulge me for a moment. If I were to write a formula for how character is formed, I would write it like this:

$$(S + P) \times O = C$$

Or

(Suffering + Patience) x Obedience = Character

I know we can't simplify character down to a formula, but when we add suffering and patience together and then multiply them by our obedience, the resulting product is Christlike character.

Obedience is a multiplier.

During times of suffering and patience, obedience produces character. God knew this when He brought the nation of Israel out of four hundred years of bondage. He used a desert, a place of testing, and a process in order to create an opportunity for the people to develop and demonstrate character:

> Be careful to follow every command I am giving you today, so that you may live and increase and may enter and possess the land the Lord promised on oath to your ancestors. Remember how the Lord your God led you all the way in the wilderness these forty years, to humble and test you in order to know what was in your heart, whether or not you would keep his commands (Deuteronomy 8:1–2, NIV).

God used the desert as an atmosphere to test character. He wanted to expose what was in the people's hearts and see if they would keep His commands. The divine detour is a place where obedience can be displayed. While God may not design all the desert places in our lives, He allows them. He wants to see what is in our hearts. He wants to see if we will obey Him.

The divine detour is a place where obedience can be displayed.

Jesus understood this truth. Many think His wilderness experience was his forty-day fast and time of temptation in the wilderness (Luke 4). The testing was actually longer. Thirty years longer to be exact. His wilderness was more than a trip through the wilds of the Galilean countryside. Instead, it was a little over thirty years, almost half a lifetime in that day. His obscurity during this time had a purpose:

> *Son though he was, he learned obedience from what he suffered (Hebrews 5:8, NIV).*

Jesus *learned* obedience. I really had difficulty with this verse when I first read it because it sounds like Jesus was once disobedient, then learned obedience over the course of time. Upon further study, I realized the word *learned* in this verse means "came to understand." Jesus came to understand what it was like to obey His Father, because He incurred suffering when He obeyed. How much suffering? The apostle Paul said:

> *And being found in appearance as a man,*
> *he humbled himself*
> *by becoming obedient to death—*
> *even death on a cross! (Philippians 2:8, NIV).*

Jesus' obedience took Him from a manger in Bethlehem to the cross at Golgotha. His obedience took Him far away from comfort, all the way to death. Your obedience to God will cause you to suffer in this life. That is true biblical suffering. It is the product of our obedience to God. Jesus learned what it was like to obey and pay the price for it by suffering through persecution, accusations, loneliness, abandonment, rejection, betrayal, and even death on a cross. It costs something to obey God. The currency of obedience is suffering. In addition, this suffering, when combined with patience, is multiplied by obedience to produce character.

> The currency of obedience is suffering. In addition, this suffering, when combined with patience, is multiplied by obedience to produce character.

Patience gives obedience time to happen. It allows us to return to the words God has spoken to us—whether through a message at church or our personal Bible study—and we choose to obey or reject them. Remember the verse we discussed earlier? James was talking about this kind of obedience when he said:

> For if you listen to the word and don't obey, it is like glancing at your face in a mirror. You see yourself, walk away, and forget what you look like. But if you look carefully into the perfect law that sets you free, and if you do what it says and don't forget what you heard, then God will bless you for doing it (James 1:23–25, NLT).

This type of obedience to the Word of God keeps us walking in the will of God. Remember, the promise of God isn't the will of God. The will of God is what you *do*, and the promise is what *inspires* us to do His will. The will of God is a walk of obedience that leads us through trials and tribulations. The result is that with every step we take on the road of His will, character is formed in us.

Disobedience, on the other hand will get us off the divine detour to God's promise. It puts us on a different path that leads to destruction and pain. However, this pain doesn't produce the kind of suffering that leads to character. It produces a suffering that leads to death. These two pathways are defined for us by Jesus when He says:

> *"Enter through the narrow gate. For wide is the gate and broad is the road that leads to destruction, and many enter through it. But small is the gate and narrow the road that leads to life, and only a few find it"* (Matthew 7:13–14, NIV).

Why do so few find and walk this pathway? Because it is camouflaged with uncomfortable circumstances. It doesn't look inviting, especially to those who are chasing a promise, want the easy way out, and don't have the patience to let character take its root and grow in their hearts. Narrow paths aren't designed for runners. A person with a fast-paced agenda will struggle on the narrow path. The path of God's will is not for the fleet-footed; it is for the sure-footed:

> *And a highway will be there;*
> *it will be called the Way of Holiness;*
> *it will be for those who walk on that Way.*
> *The unclean will not journey on it;*
> *wicked fools will not go about on it* (Isaiah 35:8, NIV).

This highway, this Way of Holiness, is paved with obedience. Isaiah also describes the location of this highway:

> *The desert and the parched land will be glad;*
> *the wilderness will rejoice and blossom.*
> *Like the crocus, it will burst into bloom;*
> *it will rejoice greatly and shout for joy.*

The glory of Lebanon will be given to it,
the splendor of Carmel and Sharon;
they will see the glory of the Lord,
the splendor of our God (Isaiah 35:1–2, NIV).

This highway is the will of God. Only those who decide to walk in obedience to the will can make the trip. They will take the road wherever the highway leads. Why does God place so much emphasis on knowing our hearts? Why does He want to know if we will obey Him when we get to our promise? Can't He just give us the promise and find out then if we will obey? The answer is, "No."

30

Beware of Praise

When wealth is lost, nothing is lost;
when health is lost, something is lost;
when character is lost, all is lost.

—Billy Graham

I loved growing up in Chipley, Florida. It was a small town with about three thousand people, and everyone knew everyone. A few people have made the trek from the simple life of Chipley to national prominence, including two athletes. One became an NBA basketball player who was selected as an all-star six times during his decorated seventeen-year career.

Another athlete was only four years my junior. He played football for a major state university in Florida and then became a star running back in the NFL. He was a good kid, who was kind, polite, and gentle to all of his classmates. Though he was extremely athletic and gifted, his older brother was even better. He was faster, bigger, and more explosive. I took physical education with his brother almost every year in high school. He was one mean dude. I remember hearing the coaches begging with him to straighten up his life, keep focused on school, and play as part of the team. But that was the problem—he didn't know how to play on a team. His ego was so inflated because of his athletic abilities that it eventually led to him being banned from sports at our high school. He could have been the next great player, like Walter Payton or Jerry Rice, but his character never matched his gift. It never came close. Years later, I read in the local newspaper that he had been killed during an altercation with police. Sad; all that talent wasted and all that potential buried.

Though an extreme example, this story illustrates how having a dream and a promise doesn't guarantee we will fulfill them. We must develop the character of Christ, if we're going to fulfill our purpose of displaying the glory of God through our gifts.

Here's an indisputable truth: Your true character *will* be revealed when the heat of your circumstances brings them to the surface. You may develop your character in privacy and obscurity, but eventually it will show itself in public. The greater the gift, the higher the platform, the more guarantee it will be displayed. That's why it is far better that your character is revealed on the training grounds of your wildernesses than in the spotlight of your Promised Land. The fall is much easier and the consequences much more manageable. If you fall on the training ground, you get up, brush yourself off, and learn from the mistake. If you fall on the battlefield, it might cost your life and maybe the lives of others.

> Here's an indisputable truth: Your true character *will* be revealed when the heat of your circumstances brings them to the surface.

My high school classmate never played in the NFL, though he had the gifts to get him there. He never made it out of the starting blocks. However, many gifted people do get started on their way. They reach great heights because they have some ethics, some character, and some discipline. However, they will eventually be challenged. Eventually their character will come into play. Eventually who they are will become public. Success is a revealer. When you succeed, you actually reveal more of who you really are.

For this reason, we need to learn obedience while we are still on our divine detour. The Promised Land isn't the place where mistakes go unnoticed. Mistakes in the Promised Land come with tremendous, often catastrophic, consequences. The Promised Land isn't a place to learn to walk in obedience; it is a place where you must walk in obedience or the promise may destroy you. Mess up in the Promised Land and people get hurt, you get hurt, reputations are destroyed, ministries collapse, and irreparable damage is done. The Promised Land is full of giant enemies, not playground tough guys. The Promised Land is a place where wars get fought; it's not a place where picnics happen. Mess up in the wilderness, and simply learn from it. Mess up in the Promised Land, and pay a steep price. Listen to the words God spoke to Joshua just after his inauguration as commander-in-chief of Israel:

> "Be strong and courageous, for you are the one who will lead these people to possess all the land I swore to their ancestors I would give them. Be strong and very courageous. Be careful to obey all the instructions Moses gave you. Do not deviate from them, turning either to the right or to the left. Then you will be successful in everything you do" (Joshua 1:6–7, NLT).

Joshua had spent forty years in the wilderness training for entry into the Promised Land. He shadowed every move Moses made. He learned, took notes, and studied. As He did, his relationship with God grew stronger (Exodus 33:11). Notice the command of

God to His new leader was to be careful to obey all the instructions and not deviate to the right or the left. Why did he need to be strong? Why did he need to be courageous? Because there was an enemy in the Promised Land, a very dangerous one.

> The Promised Land is a place where wars get fought; it's not a place where picnics happen. Mess up in the wilderness, and simply learn from it. Mess up in the Promised Land, and pay a steep price.

You might be thinking, "But I thought the promise would lead me to a wonderful place? I thought that's where the dream would be fulfilled, and my gifts would be in action?" You're correct. However, when your gifts are in action, you'll also be in a state of war against an Enemy, one who doesn't want God's glory revealed. The Enemy wants it hidden (Matthew 5:15). He wants it covered and veiled (2 Corinthians 4:4). He doesn't want you to fulfill the purposes of God while displaying the glory of God to the world. He is at war against God, and his plan is to get you to give up the promise and walk away from God's will.

If Satan can't succeed in getting you to abandon your gift, he'll try to lead you down a path that allows you to fulfill your promise without the character-building process. He'll devise shortcuts and quick routes to your dreams. The Enemy will send people your way who will express great admiration for your gift. They will exalt you for your gift without considering the character of your heart. They will celebrate your talent and place it as high as they can.

When Shannon and I were going through a major transition from a large church in the Dallas area to an itinerant traveling ministry, I went through something very similar. God had spoken to us and led me to resign as worship pastor. We began traveling, teaching, singing, and working with worship teams. It was a difficult season, definitely a wilderness journey for our family and ministry.

At times, during the first year of our pilgrimage, I received phone calls and emails from several pastors around the country who were looking for a worship pastor with the skills that had been cultivated over the previous twelve years. I remember one phone call from an optimistic, well-meaning pastor, who said, "Sion, you're everything we're looking for in a worship pastor. You're a gifted leader, and we love your heart for worship. We've listened to all your CDs." I remember when he said it that it hit me a little funny. How did he know my heart for worship? Did he really know me? He had only experienced my gift. He had only heard my talents displayed on a recording. But did he know me? Did he know my character? The answer is simple—he didn't.

After that conversation, I remembered something I once heard another well-meaning preacher say, "Go where your gifts and callings are celebrated." In other words, don't go where people don't appreciate what you can do. I thought, *"Hey, those people would celebrate me. They would celebrate my talents and gifts. That must be an open door. God wants me to go where I am celebrated!"* The moment I had that thought, those words rang in my heart and soul. God did call me to the place I am celebrated; He called me to where He leads. If that's through a wilderness with no guarantee of success, so be it. If that's to a place of obscurity, so be it. If that's to a place of serving great people instead of being a "great" person, then so be it. I would rather be in the will of God with nothing than out of God's will with everything.

I would rather be in the will of God with
nothing than out of God's will with everything.

Search the headlines of today's sports, entertainment, and national news. You will find what happens when the gifted are exalted above their character. Corrupt politicians are saying one thing to a crowd while voting the opposite on the floor of Congress. A baseball star lies about using performance-enhancing drugs. The latest teenage recording superstar has been charged with driving while intoxicated. The reality show couple is filing for divorce. The list is endless. But the church is also full of its examples. From mega churches to tiny country chapels, the mighty keep falling. Drugs, immorality, and financial scandals are almost as rampant in the church as they are in the world. Why is this so? Power corrupts. Success is a drug.

One of America's founding patriarchs, John Adams, once said, "Because power [success] corrupts, society's demands for moral authority and character increase as the importance of the position increases." Each of us has received a gift and a calling. That gift will likely lead us to a place of greater importance. That place may seem as insignificant as a physical education field in Chipley, Florida. Or it might be as significant as the Super Bowl, World Series, or the presidential debate stage. Wherever it may be, your character is vital. That's why all of us need the process. That's why we need the experience of divine detours. When the successes of this world exalt us, we need character to hold us.

31

Lures

Jesus appears to have walked unstressed and unhurried. His peaceful pace seems to imply that he measured himself not by where he was going and how fast he could get there but by whom he was following and how closely they walked together.

—*Alicia Britt Chole*

I spent a large portion of my teenage years on the front of a fishing boat. Bass fishing was my life. I was only twelve years old when I became the proud owner of my first fishing boat. Two years later, I traded it in for a larger, more productive bass boat. It was a dream come true. I don't know what it was about bass fishing that interested me so much. I liked all kinds of fishing, but none more than bass fishing. I found it challenging to catch a fish with something man-made. Unlike other types of fishing, bass fishing requires a lot strategy and deception through using plastic, wooden, and metal lures. I learned to think like a bass so I could present them with the perfect lure and trick them into biting it. The more enticing I made my presentations to the fish, the more fish I caught. It seems like a simple strategy, yet it is hard to do. Why? Because fish don't like to have metal barbs pulled through their mouths. Fish don't like being yanked from the water and placed in ice chests. Fish don't like to be fried and eaten. So how did I get them from their comfortable habitat in the water to the frying pan in my house? I had to *allure* them.

The first time I saw this verse, it reminded me of my fishing strategies:

> *"Therefore I am now going to allure her;*
> *I will lead her into the wilderness*
> *and speak tenderly to her"* (Hosea 2:14, NIV).

We've been learning about the benefits of patience in the midst of suffering. We know suffering is necessary to develop Christlike character, but how many of us would readily sign up for the next suffering session with God? If God asked, "Who wants to suffer so you can be like Jesus?" how many of us would volunteer? None of us becomes excited about that prospect.

I don't like pain. You've probably heard the saying "No pain, no gain." Well, my personal motto is more like "No pain, no pain." No pain is better than any pain. It has also been said, "Pain is weakness leaving the body." However, I say, "Pain is not for my body." So how does God get someone like me willingly to walk into a desert, a dry wilderness, without going in kicking and screaming? He *allures* me.

So how does God get someone like
me willingly to walk into a desert,
a dry wilderness, without going in
kicking and screaming? He *allures* me.

The Hebrew people who left Egypt were incredibly obstinate. Even after God miraculously delivered them from slavery, they forgot His power and doubted His goodness. Over the generations, they continued to forget about God. Through the prophet, Hosea, God spoke of Israel like an estranged wife. In order for Israel to hear Him, God first had to lead His beloved to a place of solitude, somewhere far from the idols and temptations that occupied her thoughts for such a long time.

In the same way, God lures us into this place of solitude with the bait of His promise. His divine detours take us there. Our willingness to follow shows the power of promises. They're strong enough to make even an anti-pain enthusiast such as me walk right into the wilderness, completely oblivious to the struggles ahead. I wanted the dream fulfilled. I wanted the promise in my hands. Please understand, I'm not saying God is deceitful, but He doesn't always tell us every single detail when showing us the promise. If He did, many would never sign up for it.

> God lures us into this place of solitude
> with the bait of His promise.
> His divine detours take us there.

Mothers understand this tradeoff better than anyone else does. A newly married woman often holds a new baby and thinks, "Wouldn't *this* be nice?" Then she goes home to her husband, who may not very excited about the idea at first, but he soon discovers that babies are contagious! Therefore, they decide to start trying to create a baby. Eventually, a trip to the doctor confirms their hopes—she's pregnant. For eight months, she may think, "Oh, this is going to be so wonderful," because the brain chemicals and hormones coursing through her body have fooled her. She doesn't really mind wearing her stretchy clothes, the aching back, and swollen feet. Then, week thirty-five hits and she starts thinking about the agony of the delivery room. So she begins to wonder, "What was I thinking!" But it's too late to turn back. Then, after several hours of labor, she contemplates killing her husband! In the end, after the pain, sweat, and tears, a nurse places that baby in her arms. And suddenly, it was all worth it, worth the suffering. She's willing to endure it again because of "the joy set before her":

> *Therefore, since we are surrounded by such a great cloud of witnesses, let us throw off everything that hinders and the sin that so easily entangles. And let us run with perseverance the race marked out for us, fixing our eyes on Jesus, the pioneer and perfecter of faith. For the joy set before him he endured the cross, scorning its shame, and sat down at the right hand of the throne of God. Consider him who endured such opposition from sinners, so that you will not grow weary and lose heart (Hebrews 12: 1–3, NIV).*

Jesus had His promise from the Father. The joy set before Him was that He would be resurrected and glorified, sitting at the right hand of the Father. Jesus knew that God would fulfill this promise. That knowledge sustained Him through the terrible suffering He endured. He understood the path of suffering better than His closest friends, who thought the path to glory could only be glorious. Peter rebuked Jesus because he couldn't believe that the Son of Man should have to suffer (Matt. 16:22). However, Jesus knew God's will for Him included intense suffering followed by an unjust death. He also knew the Father's promise—that His suffering and death would reveal God's glory.

Remember, Jesus Himself promised we would suffer in His name and for His cause. As we have already discussed, the apostle Peter wrote to the churches who were suffering persecution, "Dear friends, do not be surprised at the painful trial you are suffering, as though something strange were happening to you" (1 Pet. 4:12, NIV). We must not be taken by surprise when evil afflicts God's people. Instead, we have to remain patient through the suffering and allow God to use those circumstances for our good. Patient endurance often gives us a greater capacity for God's blessing later. Peter continues, "but rejoice inasmuch as you participate in the sufferings of Christ, so that you may be overjoyed when his glory is revealed" (1 Peter 4:13, NIV). By transforming our character now, God prepares us for a future so good, so abundantly positive, that we can barely imagine the joy.

> Patient endurance often gives us a
> greater capacity for God's blessing later.

God *wants* to bless you, as long as those blessings will not destroy you. In order to prepare you for long-term blessing, He must make you ready through short-term suffering. While these circumstances are difficult, you will look back one day and say with Him, "The suffering was not only necessary, it was also a small sacrifice for the blessings I enjoy now."

My hope is that you are reading this book because you sense that God has joy waiting for you in the future. You believe God has placed within you a dream, a sense of purpose you long to experience. If so, you're probably beginning to discover that fulfilling the dream requires counting the cost. If you're like many people, you sense Him calling you to follow Him into the wilderness, but you're wondering if it's the right move. Maybe you're thinking it's not worth it. He may ask you to move your family, go back to school, learn a new skill, or trust Him with your finances. Still, He's luring you; He's calling you to relinquish those things that you currently hold dear and trust Him completely. Go ahead. Take the bait. You won't regret it!

32
Silence

Jesus appears to have walked unstressed and unhurried. His peaceful pace seems to imply that he measured himself not by where he was going and how fast he could get there but by whom he was following and how closely they walked together.

—*Alicia Britt Chole*

It was a hard, long season. I knew we were in a desert, a wilderness place to be sure. It was a divine detour to end all detours. God had spoken and made a promise. Shannon and I stepped out in obedience to God's will. We knew we were destined for a time of testing. Finances were tight. Real tight. I was traveling around the country teaching and singing during this time, waiting on God to open a door to a place where our dreams could be fulfilled. I didn't know where that place was, but I knew I'd recognize it when I saw it.

Much prayer had led us here. In the early stages of this journey, the Lord's voice was clear and direct, offering us guidance to what we believed would be a quick transition. We didn't realize how wrong we were. What followed those initial instructions was something I wasn't prepared for and hadn't really experienced in my walk with God: *Silence.* Specifically, silence from God. No matter how much I prayed . . . silence. No matter how long I fasted . . . silence.

"Hey God, it's me, Sion!" *Silence.*

"Remember me? I'm the one You told to quit my full-time job as a pastor and wait for the next order from You." *Silence.*

"What do You want me to do now?" *Silence.*

"Where should we move and what church should we join forces with?" *Silence.*

"Hey God, the bills are piling up." *Silence.*

Silence. Silence. Silence.

After several months of silence from God, I did what every Christian probably would do. I started questioning if I had actually heard from God. So I repented. God responded with more *silence.* I went as far as repenting for sins I never committed just in case I forgot something. The result? *Silence.*

Frustrated and confused, I found myself sitting on an airplane travelling to another speaking engagement in another state. A friend I hadn't seen in years happened to sit down beside me. He was a traveling evangelist on his way back from a ministry event. After the usual small talk that happens between two friends who haven't seen each other in a while, he asked how I was doing. And I was honest with him:

"I haven't heard from God in almost nine months. I pray and wait to hear His voice and I hear nothing. It's as if He's not speaking. I go to these meetings and God blesses people when I teach and sing. Many of them actually hear the Lord speak through me, but I can't seem to hear God speak to me. He's totally silent."

"Sounds to me like you're in a test," said my friend.

"Duh. No kidding," I responded. "I just wish He would say something. Tell us what to do. That's all I ask. If He'll just speak, we'll obey. It couldn't get any worse that it was."

I'll never forget the next words my friend spoke to me. They turned my world upside-down. He spoke wisdom that unlocked the doors to the treasures of walking in God's perfect will:

"Sion, the teacher doesn't talk during a test," he said.

Whoa! That was it. If anyone should have known this, it should have been me! I was a professional college student at one time. I spent nine years in college, and I knew all about tests and classroom etiquette. Teachers don't talk during tests. They don't teach when the multiple-choice questions are sitting in front of the student. The teaching is over, and the teacher places the test there to find out if the student learned something during the class. No wonder God was silent during this season. I was in a test!

Teachers don't talk during tests.

Those words of revelation revolutionized the way I walked through the rest of that season. I realized God wasn't being silent because He was cruel. He wasn't quiet because I had missed His will. He wanted to know what was in my heart, if I would do what I had already learned. Does that remind you of a verse we looked at earlier?

Remember how the Lord your God led you all the way in the wilderness these forty years, to humble and test you in order to know what was in your heart, whether or not you would keep his commands (Deuteronomy 8:2, NIV).

The wilderness is an exam. The detour is an essay. It's not a time when the teacher stands at the podium and lectures the class. God's tests are proof the lesson has already been taught. They're evidence that promotion is near. Our responses will determine whether we graduate and move on or not. Fail the test, repeat the class. Pass the test, move on to the next level.

God only tests us on the things that He already taught us.

God only tests us on the things that He already taught us. Wouldn't it be cruel for a teacher to hand out a test on something in the lesson plan for the *next* week? That would not be a good or fair teacher. But if you're in a test, He has already taught you what you need to know. You already have the answers; you just need to remember the lesson. Remember that sermon. Remember that Bible study. Remember that devotional. Remember that holy experience.

And God's tests are *open book tests*! You can *always* use your notes! You can get out the textbook and look up the answers. When God is silent, when the Teacher isn't teaching, get out your notes and open the textbook (Bible). Use what He has already taught you to get through this difficult season. His Word, spoken to you in the past, will guide you through what you're going through today.

> *All Scripture is inspired by God and is useful to teach us what is true and to make us realize what is wrong in our lives. It corrects us when we are wrong and teaches us to do what is right. God uses it to prepare and equip his people to do every good work (2 Timothy 3:16–17, NLT).*

When I'm teaching about this process, sometimes I warn my audience. I caution them that we'll be tested on what we've been taught. Every sermon we hear, every book we read, every Bible study class we attend will determine the tests we take one day. God wants to know if what you've heard and read is in your heart. He wants to know if you really believe His Word. So He administers an exam to see if we really know and believe His Word.

God's tests are *open book tests*!
You can *always* use your notes!

God doesn't design tests and trials to teach us. That's not their purpose. They are intended to *reveal* what we already know. Tests and trials don't develop character; they disclose character. Yes, God develops character in us during our wilderness experiences, but that character is also tested. Character is displayed during desert times—either in abundance or in lack. Character development has either occurred or not occurred. It's the purpose of the test to find out.

I made many mistakes during that particular wilderness experience. I failed some of those tests. Yes, I passed some, but I also failed some. Those that I failed proved that I needed more instruction and classroom time. Now that I have retaken some of the classes, I realize I really did know the correct answers during the first tests, but I just didn't do what God's Word says to do. Sometimes I found out that it wasn't in my heart, it was only in my head. The tests proved it.

However, I also learned something else: You're supposed to go *through* deserts, not live in them. In God's original plan, Israel would pass through the desert and then enter the Promised Land, but they didn't. At the border of receiving their promise, they fell back into their old ways of doubt and self-reliance. They hadn't mastered the lessons from their experiences with the Red Sea, the golden calf, the manna, the water from the rock, and the many other examples of God's power and faithfulness to fulfill His promises. Their test at Kadesh Barnea (Numbers 13) revealed that they weren't yet ready to possess the Land of Promise. God had brought them out of Egypt practically kicking and screaming. When they arrived at the threshold of "the land of milk and honey," God wasn't going to bring them *in* kicking and screaming. The blessing of the Promised Land would have led to their undoing, so they had to repeat a grade. Back into the wilderness, they went for forty years of training.

You're supposed to go *through* deserts, not live in them.

I know many people who've spent decades in the desert, circling mountains, wandering around so long they could be "tour guides" to the wilderness. They adopt the idea that the wilderness is their destination, and they settle in while blaming their surroundings on everyone and everything but themselves. Deserts are for seasons, not for lifetimes. There is nothing you can do to shorten the time you spend in the wilderness. There is nothing you can do to decrease the amount of time you spend wandering. That time is set by the Teacher. You can, however, increase the time you spend in the desert. You can spend eleven days or forty years. The choice is yours. How you respond to the tests will determine the length of the divine detour.

33

Intoxicated

Alas, how much pride have the best of us in our hearts! It is the worst part of the body of sin and death, the first sin that ever entered into the universe, and the last that is rooted out. It is God's most stubborn enemy.

—Jonathan Edwards

Just as we know God wants to allure us into the wilderness to be refined by Him, we can be equally sure Satan also wants to lure us. He desires to entice us away from the will of God and, ultimately, from fulfilling the dream that God has placed in our hearts. He doesn't want us to walk obediently in the will of God and reach the promises the Father has given.

As we discussed earlier, God's will often does *not look* like His promises. As we walk in the will of God during these times, we can be very susceptible to the Enemy's lures and traps. Satan knows this and uses a rather predictable tactic to get us off the pathway of God's will. His lures *appear* to be godly fulfillments of our dream. He's smart enough to disguise the steely barbs of evil as something good. Then he drags the lure across our paths. He is, after all, the "father of all lies," so he doesn't tempt us to give up the promise or abandon the dream altogether. Rather, he entices us to pursue *the dream* instead of the *Dream Giver*, bypassing the processes of God and jumping on the fast track to the promise. Satan wants us to pursue the promise *on our own terms*, which he knows will undermine God's plans and eventually lead to our destruction.

We can avoid chasing Satan's lures by submitting to God's Word and will, day-by-day, moment-by-moment, allowing Him to transform our character through perseverance, and consciously cultivating a lifestyle of obedience. As we persevere through trials as Christ did, we see what God has made of us and gain confidence in our deepening character. Because victory begets victory, the test gives us greater courage to overcome future temptation.

But there is more to being Christlike than simply learning to choose obedience over taking the easy way out. We not only struggle with our unwillingness to wait patiently in the will of God, we must also face a problem that lies deep in the heart of every person—*pride*.

I think of pride as the *soil* from which all sin grows. Out of pride comes all kinds of vices, often disguised in the regal, self-righteous robes of good intentions. As you may recall, Satan's downfall resulted from his own arrogance and vainglory. His first temptation to the angels that eventually followed him appealed to their pride—the notion they could be as great as or better than their Maker could. Satan's temptation continues to cast the illusion of self-sufficiency, drawing us away from the Father who has all the best planned for us. This pride drives people to reject God while acknowledging His sovereignty and goodness with their lips.

We read often about pride in Scripture. I think it's because it caused the downfall of many who God used otherwise in incredible ways. A good example can be found in the story of King Uzziah in 2 Chronicles 26. He ascended to the throne of Judah at only sixteen. Imagine a sixteen-year-old ruling over a nation!

Uzziah began reasonably well. Unlike many of his predecessors in both Judah and Israel, he followed the guidance of godly advisors:

Uzziah was sixteen years old when he became king, and he reigned in Jerusalem fifty-two years. His mother's name was Jekoliah; she was from Jerusalem. He did what was right in the eyes of the Lord, just as his father Amaziah had done. He sought God during the days of Zechariah, who instructed him in the fear of God. As long as he sought the Lord, God gave him success (2 Chronicles 26:3–5, NIV).

But after several years of success on the battlefield and wise dealings in the court, he soon met an enemy he hadn't prepared for. This is the enemy that eventually destroyed him.

In Jerusalem he made devices invented for use on the towers and on the corner defenses so that soldiers could shoot arrows and hurl large stones from the walls. His fame spread far and wide, for he was greatly helped until he became powerful.

    But after Uzziah became powerful, his pride led to his downfall. He was unfaithful to the Lord his God, and entered the temple of the Lord to burn incense on the altar of incense. Azariah the priest with eighty other courageous priests of the Lord followed him in. They confronted King Uzziah and said, "It is not right for you, Uzziah, to burn incense to the Lord. That is for the priests, the descendants of Aaron, who have been consecrated to burn incense. Leave the sanctuary, for you have been unfaithful; and you will not be honored by the Lord God."

    Uzziah, who had a censer in his hand ready to burn incense, became angry. While he was raging at the priests in their presence before the incense altar in the Lord's temple, leprosy broke out on his forehead (2 Chronicles 26:15–19, NIV).

Even though you've never been a monarch, your gifts will elevate you in one way or another, especially if they equip you for leadership or some other kind of public role. If you're especially talented, you should know God has prepared to elevate you. Like King Uzziah, other people may celebrate you for your gift. The extent of your elevation may be around the world, across the country, across your town, through your church, or in your own home. Wherever and however it may be, you're going to have some success. So beware . . . that success can fuel pride like gasoline on a fire.

In some ways, it's hard to blame Uzziah. He simply wanted to worship the Lord personally in His temple without an intermediary. Nevertheless, God had established a priestly system to serve as the proper way to approach Him. Uzziah's pride convinced him that he didn't need to follow God's orders. Pride, sustained by his power and success, fooled him into thinking he had outgrown his need for the priesthood, that his life of fame exempted him from needing consecration. Up until that point, God had rewarded Uzziah's faithfulness. That Lord gave him success and fame, but when Uzziah's pride blinded him so badly that his own worship turned to rebellion, God did not hesitate to act. Uzziah lived the rest of his life separate from others, bearing the consequences of his downfall all over his face. Even more, his leprosy kept him from ever setting foot in the Temple again.

Where did Uzziah go wrong? At what point did he replace submission with lifting up himself? When did he begin thinking he was great and powerful? I don't think Uzziah woke up one morning and suddenly believed that his strength and his power all came from his own efforts. Instead, I believe it happened gradually and progressively. It was a process.

In the opening verses of the story, sixteen-year-old Uzziah sought the Lord. He submitted to the prophet Zechariah and learned the ways of God. His first steps were humble ones. He walked in God's will and character grew in the young ruler's heart. However, something accompanied Uzziah's success—his heart *became proud*. These same words describe Lucifer just before his fall from heaven:

Your heart became proud
  on account of your beauty,
and you corrupted your wisdom
  because of your splendor.
So I threw you to the earth;
  I made a spectacle of you before kings (Ezekiel 28:17, NIV).

Let me be blunt: Success is an *intoxicant*. Ministry leaders, business people, athletes, musicians, and many others reach a place in their professions when success arrives and pride sets in like a cancer. I have seen it repeatedly. Some who fell to its poison were close to me and others I saw at a distance, but the result was the same: pride set in when success was realized.

Let me be blunt: success is an *intoxicant*.

Don't be fooled by thinking you have to win the lottery of success before pride begins to intoxicate you. I've seen it happen in ministries I would call successful on a small scale. It doesn't have to be world-changing success for it to become poison in the organization or person. Everyone views success differently. What may make my head swell with pride may not impress someone else. Nevertheless, success can become an intoxicant. That is what happened in Uzziah's life, but it doesn't take being a monarch before pride's poison can spoil your walk with God.

Somewhere along the line, Uzziah took the bait. Sometime in his early reign, the snare of the Enemy led him away from God's will. He pursued the promise of being the greatest king in Israel since his ancestor David. He left the pathway of God's will and took a more attractive route to the promise. He bypassed broken-ness and headed straight into the direction of instant fame and fortune. He no longer needed Zechariah's wisdom and oversight. He didn't seek the Lord for answers. Uzziah thought *he* was strong, but he forgot that the Lord gave him that success.

So how can we protect ourselves against this lure of pride, the same sin as Lucifer? How can we recognize the Enemy's scheme and safeguard our hearts against the intoxicating effects of success? We need to have a better understanding of what caused the original fall of creation and humanity—pride.

34

Before a Fall

If I had only one sermon to preach, it would be a sermon against pride.

—G. K. Chesterton

Sun Tzu, the ancient Chinese military sage, wrote in *The Art of War*, "If you know the enemy and know yourself, you need not fear the result of a hundred battles"(Sun Tzu, 2009, 115). Since pride is one of the greatest weapons of the Enemy, we must study it well. It's not enough to be aware of pride or keep it at a safe distance. We must expose its deadly inner workings with accurate knowledge and aggressive confrontation. And the best way to learn about pride is to look at its origins.

Pride and its devastating effects go back to the very beginning, even before God created this world. Pride took root in the heart of one of God's most beautiful creatures—Lucifer. Earlier, we looked at the function and purpose of this archangel, and learned his job description consisted of reflecting and refracting the glory of God by way of the gifts placed inside of him. We don't know how long Lucifer served in the presence of God. It could have been millions of years, but we don't know. What we do know is at some point during his tenure as a cherubim, pride developed in his heart due to his beauty and splendor:

Your heart became proud
  on account of your beauty,
and you corrupted your wisdom
  because of your splendor.
So I threw you to the earth;
  I made a spectacle of you before kings (Ezekiel 28:17, NIV).

Many people wonder why God created Satan. They wonder why a good and just God would create a creature so evil. Well, God didn't. He created Lucifer, not Satan. He created an archangel who was beautiful, perfect, and without fault. Lucifer created Satan when he allowed the accolades he received to plant a seed in his heart into the soil of pride.

Many traditionally credit Lucifer as being heaven's worship leader during this time. This account is not entirely accurate. Lucifer was only an instrument used by heaven's worship leader— God (Neese, 2014). Lucifer was an instrument in the hands of the Master. He simply displayed the glory of God through the gifts and instruments that were a part of his being.

But at some point, Lucifer began to think the praise and adoration was directed towards him, rather than God. His wisdom became corrupt and self-gratifying, meaning that his thoughts were now corrupted, and he thought *he* was the source of beauty to whom creation responded. Until that point, he was blameless:

You were blameless in your ways
  from the day you were created
  till wickedness was found in you (Ezekiel 28:15, NIV).

Notice it was "wickedness" that was found, rather than pride. I am going to step out here and make a bold statement based on some conclusions I've come to about pride. I don't believe the Bible directly condemns pride as a sin. I can't find it in the Scripture. In its purest form, to be proud or have pride in something is to "have delight or elation arising from some act, possession, or relationship." Feeling delight because your kids are well-behaved or because you received a big promotion at work isn't a sin. Scripture even encourages pride when it says:

> Believers in humble circumstances ought to take pride in their high position. But the rich should take pride in their humiliation—since they will pass away like a wild flower (James 1:9–10, NIV).

I'm not saying God doesn't deal with the proud and the prideful. Proverbs 8:13 says that God, "hates pride and arrogance," and James 4:6 says that God "opposes the proud but gives grace to the humble." The Greek word "opposes" literally means "to resist with force." It's a military term that describes pushing an enemy back from the position they are occupying. God resists those who harbor pride in their hearts.

Nevertheless, pride didn't get Lucifer kicked out of heaven. Wickedness did. Rebellion did.

Nevertheless, pride didn't get Lucifer kicked out of heaven. Wickedness did. Rebellion did. It wasn't until the pride in his heart bore fruit that he incurred God's wrath. Pride could have been in his heart for years, but until it manifested, business went on as usual. He demonstrated the wickedness in his heart when his corrupted wisdom led him to believe he was like God:

> "How you are fallen from heaven,
> O Lucifer, son of the morning!

How you are cut down to the ground,
You who weakened the nations!
For you have said in your heart:
'I will ascend into heaven,
I will exalt my throne above the stars of God;
I will also sit on the mount of the congregation
On the farthest sides of the north;
I will ascend above the heights of the clouds,
I will be like the Most High"' (Isaiah 14:12–14, NKJV).

The pride in his heart led to rebellion. That rebellion quickly got him kicked out of heaven. Again, pride didn't get Lucifer kicked out, rebellion did. Pride was the soil in which wickedness and rebellion grew. Even so, pride wasn't developed or cultivated in an environment of evil. In fact, it was conceived in the very throne room of God with the glory of God emanating and radiating. It was built, grain by grain, in the heart of God's instrument of worship as creation responded to the glory that was revealed through Lucifer. Ezekiel 28:18 describes this action as "dishonest trade" or "merchandising." In other words, Lucifer received profit, praise, and adoration that he didn't rightly own. The worship of creation was meant to pass through Lucifer and back to God. Instead, he kept it for himself and didn't return it to God.

That was the sin of "merchandising."

The soil of pride gave birth to sin—the first sin. It also gave birth to humanity's first fatal sin when this fallen angel, Satan, told Eve that she "would not surely die" if she ate from the Tree of the Knowledge of Good and Evil. The serpent successfully planted his seed of deception in the prideful heart of God's most cherished possession. Just like in Lucifer, pride gave way to the sin of rebellion as Adam and Eve traded their rightful position as God's ambassadors to "be like God, knowing good and evil" (Genesis 3:1–5).

Sin needs an atmosphere in which to grow, and pride is the perfect incubator.

Just as the soil in a garden gives nutrients and nourishment to the plants, pride sustains the seeds it hosts. It provides the perfect environment for the seeds of sin and stability for the plant once it grows. Sin needs an atmosphere in which to grow, and pride is the perfect incubator.

35

P.R.I.D.E.

Pride is when sinful human beings aspire to the status and position of God and refuse to acknowledge their dependence upon Him.

—C.J Mahaney

Now that we've discovered pride is the soil in which sin grows, let's look at the nature of pride. What makes it so destructive? I've tried to make it easy to remember by creating an acrostic from the word P.R.I.D.E.

Powerful
Never underestimate the destructive power of pride. Pride has taken down greater men and women than you or me, such as King Uzziah. Pride has ruined people who knew the Scriptures. It has destroyed some of the most dedicated servants of God, including those who rose to the top of their fields. Proverbs clearly states: "Pride goes before destruction, and a haughty spirit before a fall" (Proverbs16:18, NIV).

Over many years of full-time ministry, sadly, I've encountered some people with an amazing amount of pride. I've thought to myself, *"How in the world is God still using these people!"* Then, in quiet moments, the Holy Spirit reminds me that one day, in the absence of repentance, those people will fall. And if I'm not careful, I could stumble as well. I have seen at least ten once-successful ministries crash and burn because of pride. None of those leaders ever said, "I'm so full of pride, one day I'm going to fall." No, instead the success they experienced intoxicated them and they thought they could do no wrong.

I was in a meeting once with a very arrogant leader. His church had grown rapidly over a period of two years. Hundreds were being saved every weekend. When a question arose during the meeting that challenged a decision he had recently made, his response was, "How could I be wrong? If God's blessing wasn't on me and this ministry, we wouldn't be seeing all these people come to Christ!"

This man made a grave error in his observation.

He was drunk with success.

He was so inebriated that his "wisdom was corrupted" to the point where he mistakenly thought God's presence in a service was God's approval of this leader's character and lifestyle. God's presence in your life and ministry is *not* necessarily God's approval of your life and ministry. People were responding because God's Word was being preached in those services. God's Word never returns without effect (Isaiah 55:11).

This man had mistaken signs and wonders with *fruit*.

God's presence in your life and ministry
is *not* necessarily God's approval
of your life and ministry.

Jesus told us we should judge a tree by its fruit (Matthew 12:33). He didn't say we should judge the tree by its signs and wonders. In fact, Jesus said on the Day of Judgment many would discover the emptiness of miracles without fruit:

> *Many will say to me on that day, 'Lord, Lord, did we not prophesy in your name and in your name drive out demons and in your name perform many miracles?' Then I will tell them plainly, 'I never knew you. Away from me, you evildoers!' (Matthew 7:22–23, NIV).*

Clearly, signs and wonders followed these evildoers. They didn't, however, possess the fruit of a good tree.

So what is this fruit? The Bible says it is "love, joy, peace, patience, kindness, gentleness, faithfulness and self-control" (Galatians 5:22–23). The arrogant leader I mentioned saw great signs and wonders in his ministry, but he lacked fruit. There was very little self-control, kindness, or gentleness. On the contrary, his ministry was filled with quite the opposite, and soon it declined and fell into obscurity.

> Jesus told us we should judge a tree by its fruit (Matthew 12:33). He didn't say we should judge the tree by its signs and wonders.

We see the plague of pride infecting leaders all across history. Hezekiah, another king of Judah, became proud and brought the wrath of God upon himself, his city, and his nation (2 Chronicles 32:25–26). The pride of Nebuchadnezzar reduced him to roaming a field and eating grass like an animal for several years (Daniel 4:30–33). Herod Agrippa refused to give God glory and accepted the worship of his subjects, which led to him being eaten by worms from the inside out and then dying a humiliating death (Acts 12:21–23).

Religious

"The chief mark of counterfeit holiness is its lack of humility," said Andrew Murray in *Humility and Absolute Surrender* (Murray, 2012, 27). Murray also stated, "There is no pride so dangerous, because none so subtle and insidious, as the pride of holiness." Some of the most prideful and arrogant people I have ever met were clothed in religious pomp. Their religiosity was a sham, a cloak, a covering for what was really beneath the surface.

Sadly, pride and a religious spirit make for a perfect pairing. Perhaps the most notorious example appears during Jesus' ministry as He repeatedly rebuked a group of religious experts known as the Pharisees. Today, we likely think of the Pharisees as buffoons, so overly religious they hardly seem real. In reality, they weren't much different from people we know today. The Pharisees were highly respected, because they dedicated their lives to following perfectly all the Old Testament laws. They even added a long list of customs and traditions to the Law of Moses, which they followed to the letter, and required the same of others.

Jesus was adamantly opposed to their religious piety. He spoke directly to this group when He told this parable:

> "Two men went up to the temple to pray, one a Pharisee and the other a tax collector. The Pharisee stood by himself and prayed: 'God, I thank you that I am not like other people—robbers, evildoers, adulterers—or even like this tax collector. I fast twice a week and give a tenth of all I get.'
>
> "But the tax collector stood at a distance. He would not even look up to heaven, but beat his breast and said, 'God, have mercy on me, a sinner.'
>
> "I tell you that this man, rather than the other, went home justified before God. For all those who exalt themselves will be humbled, and those who humble themselves will be exalted" (*Luke 18:10–14, NIV*).

Again, in another discussion with the Pharisees, Jesus confronted their religious pride:

> *"Woe to you, teachers of the law and Pharisees, you hypocrites!*
> *You clean the outside of the cup and dish, but inside they are*
> *full of greed and self-indulgence. Blind Pharisee! First clean the*
> *inside of the cup and dish, and then the outside also will be clean"*
> *(Matthew 23:25–26, NIV).*

Why does pride lead to more religiosity? It's because religious activity functions as a sedative to quiet the turmoil raging on the inside of the proud heart. Dogmatic condemnation and superiority need a sedative, because deep inside a prideful, religious person is miserable. They realize their own shortcomings, but they would never admit them, nor let anyone know the true state of their spirituality.

> Why does pride lead to more religiosity?
> It's because religious activity functions as
> a sedative to quiet the turmoil raging
> on the inside of the proud heart.

How do I know all this? Because I've personally walked in religious pride. I know what it feels like to sing something on Sunday and live something else on Monday morning. Instead of confronting the painful reality of my true, prideful condition, I let my religious actions become my sedative. I tore others down to make myself feel better. Because God opposes the proud, I felt resisted and pushed away by Him. I needed a fix of His presence; but instead, I painted the outside to cover the dirty inside.

King Uzziah likely felt this. His quest for power and success left him empty and hungry for true connection with God. This eventually drove him to God. He went to the Temple, attempting to worship. However, with a pride-infested heart, he sought God on his own terms, not God's. He thought he was above the commands of God. His action illustrates a core characteristic of pride—self-exaltation to a place only God can and should occupy. He thought he was God's equal and could approach Him on Uzziah's terms. The priests in the Temple courageously confronted the king about his prideful actions:

> *They confronted King Uzziah and said, "It is not right for you, Uzziah, to burn incense to the Lord. That is for the priests, the descendants of Aaron, who have been consecrated to burn incense. Leave the sanctuary, for you have been unfaithful; and you will not be honored by the Lord God."*
>
> *Uzziah, who had a censer in his hand ready to burn incense, became angry. While he was raging at the priests in their presence before the incense altar in the Lord's temple, leprosy broke out on his forehead (2 Chronicles 26:18–19, NIV).*

Uzziah became defensive and angry, because he thought of himself as equal with God and above other people. He thought more highly of himself than he actually was. This response always follows religious pride.

Religious acts of pride also manifest themselves under the guise of false humility—self-deprecating humor or self-condemning declarations around others. The Lord confronted me on this issue several years into full-time ministry. After a worship service, people would come up to me and say, "Oh Sion, you know when you sang that song, it just ministered to me and blessed me so much!" I gave the expected response, "Well, praise be to God. Glory to Him and Christ only." While I sounded religious and humble, inside I was thinking, "Say some more, say some more." I liked it! I would even go into the church lobby after services just to get a pat on the back, especially after a great service. I was responding with false humility.

God soon confronted me on this issue after a service where I totally blew it. I messed up something and made a complete idiot of myself in front of the whole congregation. In reality, no one probably noticed it, but I knew it and felt horrible. After the service, I sat in the room backstage after the service and refused to go into the lobby. I couldn't face anyone. They wouldn't be giving me a pat on the back or encouragement, so I didn't want to go out there. That's when I felt God asking me why. In a moment of honesty, I told Him it was because I had messed up. Then it hit me. The only reason I ever went out there was to get praise. It was about me. It was false humility.

I realized then that false humility is one of the most dangerous forms of pride. It's religious and pious. It clothes itself in false motives and cliché answers to those who seek to encourage and thank us. So what do I say now when people thank me for a service or special moment during worship? I simply say, "Thank you." I know who touched their hearts, and it certainly wasn't me.

> I realized then that false humility is one
> of the most dangerous forms of pride.

I gained an important revelation about something that day. If I take credit for my failures, I will inevitably take credit for my victories. People who are constantly self-deprecating and hard on themselves when they blow it will always take the credit when they hit it right on the mark. It's proof that we have wrapped our identity in our performance. That is false humility. And it is religious pride.

> If I take credit for my failures, I will
> inevitably take credit for my victories.

Insidious

Pride is insidious, which is actually a medical term. One dictionary definition says it is "a disease developing so gradually as to be well established before becoming apparent." That's what pride is—a spiritual disease, a debilitating condition of the soul that if left undetected and untreated, it results in catastrophe for the prideful person and all those intimately connected to that individual. Unfortunately, we're born with this disease. It's congenital, passed down to us from our parents. From the time we are born, the symptoms become apparent to everyone but us. It grows especially quickly in darkness, because it cannot bear exposure to light. Many people remain unaware of this disease or how quickly it can take over until it brings them to a stunning, tragic end. Even when that ending is catastrophic, the underlying cause of the fall often goes undiagnosed, while blame is shifted and hearts are further hardened.

Think of how many times you've seen a secret sin exposed in a high-profile minister. The sin may go back many years, even while that person's ministry was at its peak of influence. Throughout that time, God was always present in the ministry, shouting warnings in ears deafened by pride. But in the end, in the absence of repentance, the minister fell.

Deceptive

Through pride we are ever deceiving ourselves. But deep down below the surface of the average conscience a still, small voice says to us, something is out of tune.

—Carl Jung

One of the most disturbing and detrimental aspects of pride is how it deceives its host. People with pride don't know they have it. When confronted about it, prideful people readily deny the existence of it in their hearts. They don't know it's there because it's deceptive! Obadiah addressed this problem when he said, "The pride of your heart has deceived you" (Obadiah verse 3). Jeremiah declared, "The terror you inspire and the pride in your heart have deceived you" (Jeremiah 49:16). Pride deceives the heart of its host, and because it's insidious, it can grow without knowledge. The combination of the two makes it all the more dangerous!

So how do we know if we have pride? In two ways: First, if you don't think you have it, you are probably full of it. Second, ask someone. I tell people that pride is like bad breath—everyone knows you have it but you!

Everyone

He is a modest little man who has a good deal to be modest about.
　　　　　—Winston Churchill (describing a political opponent).

That brings us to the final letter of our acrostic. Pride affects everyone. No one is immune. When the first people disobeyed God in the Garden of Eden and introduced sin to the world, human nature became corrupt. Pride now drives many of the decisions we make, including the choice to fulfill our own divine promise and make our own dream come true. We all struggle with the temptation to impose our own will rather than trust God to do things His way and according to His schedule.

The good news is that God has a solution to the universal problem of pride. While the Bible encourages us to humble ourselves (James 4:10; 1 Peter 3:6), the Lord hasn't left us alone in our struggle. He not only sent His Son to be our example, but He has also given every believer the Holy Spirit to live within them. That's why He uses *all* of our experiences, including times in the divine detour and seasons of affliction, to cure the disease and remove the soil of pride from our hearts.

Chapter 36
The Great Compass

*God created the world out of nothing, and as long as we are noth-
ing, He can make something out of us.*

—*Martin Luther*

As we noted previously, the journey from the promise given
to the promise fulfilled is all about *change*. It's the reason the
Holy Spirit leads us on divine detours. God wants to bring about a
change in our lives. He wants us to become more like the *doxa* we
see in the mirror of the promise. Instead of spending our efforts
and time trying to change our surroundings and other people
around us, we need to let God work in our hearts to bring about
this change. And the agent God uses to change us is *grace*. With
grace, you will change. Without grace, you will never change.

People in the church tend to toss the word *grace* around freely,
but few actually know the meaning of this amazing gift. Even fewer
have experienced grace themselves. Many people think of grace as
a get-out-of-jail-free card. On the other hand, maybe it's a camou-
flage covering God throws over sin to keep from seeing it. I've had
people tell me right in front of the altar, "Well, you know, if it wasn't
for the grace of God, I'd probably split hell wide open." No, what
you are actually describing is not grace but *mercy*.

Many have rolled those two words, "grace" and "mercy," into one
definition. I have heard the two words used interchangeably many

times in Christian circles. However, grace and mercy are quite different. I love how simply my pastor, Robert Morris, explains it, "Mercy occurs when you don't get what you deserve. Grace occurs when get what you don't deserve."

My definition of mercy is a little more subtle: "I'm still breathing." I don't deserve life, especially eternal life, but God has given it to me instead of the death I deserved.

Grace is getting what I don't deserve. What I don't deserve is a way out of the sin that imprisons me. Grace doesn't excuse or overlook sin. Grace is the power of God to overcome sin. Grace brings about change.

> Grace doesn't excuse or overlook sin.
> Grace is the power of God to overcome sin.
> Grace brings about change.

I went through almost eighteen years of my Christian life without understanding these things about grace. Like many people, I thought grace did the job of excusing or covering up my sins. However, the apostle Paul asks this question:

What shall we say, then? Shall we go on sinning so that grace may increase? (Romans 6:1, NIV).

The answer is "No!" His question would be like asking, "Should I get sick so I can take some more yummy medicine?" That would be ridiculous! Grace isn't a license or a free ticket to sin; grace brings the power of God into our lives to help us *overcome* sin.

So how does grace do this? How does it bring about change in our lives? To find the answer, we need to look no further than Jesus Himself:

The Word became flesh and made his dwelling among us. We have seen his glory, the glory of the one and only son, who came from the Father, full of grace and truth (John 1:14, NIV).

Jesus came *full of grace and truth.* It was a package deal—grace and truth. For grace to fulfill its purpose in each of our lives, truth must be present. The same applies with truth. For it to have impact in our lives, we need the grace to live what truth demands. Grace without truth leads to runaway sin. Truth without grace leads to legalism. Grace and truth go hand in hand, balanced by God's mercy at the fulcrum.

Grace is the power of God helping us do what truth demands. Not only does God give us truth to set us free, He also gives us the power to do what that truth demands so that we can be free. Wow! What a wonderful God! That's what makes grace so amazing! Paul described the same power:

> *For God is working in you, giving you the desire and the power to do what pleases him (Philippians 2:13 NLT).*

How do we receive this grace? Do we simply pray and ask God for it? Once again, look at these words from the author of Hebrews:

> *Let us then approach God's throne of grace with confidence, so that we may receive mercy and find grace to help us in our time of need (Hebrews 4:16, NIV).*

The first way we receive grace is by coming before God. Based on this verse, mercy is something we *receive*, but grace is something we *find*. Mercy is given and so it must be received. Grace is hidden and so it must be found.

Grace is the power of God helping us do what truth demands.

Where do we find grace? Look at the name of the God's throne. It's the "throne of grace"! His grace is found at His throne. His throne is called *grace*! Where His Lordship and Kingship is in our lives, that's where we'll find grace. Wherever His throne resides, grace is there. If there are places in our hearts where He isn't Lord, no grace can be found (remember the idol chapter). This is further illustrated when God said of Moses:

". . . you have found grace in my sight" (Exodus 33:17, NKJV).

The Bible also says this about Noah:

But Noah found grace in the eyes of the Lord (Genesis 6:8, NKJV).

Both of these verses reveal that if we find God's face, we find God's grace. It's that simple.

> If we find God's face, we find God's grace.
> It's that simple.

So how do we find the face of God? We need a compass. The compass God uses in our hearts is called humility. Humility keeps us on God's divine detour, the perfect path of God's will. It keeps us from bypassing the process to get to our promises.

As I mentioned earlier, I love the outdoors. To an outdoorsman, nothing is more valuable for navigating than a compass. It keeps us going in the right direction. It doesn't show us where the destination is, rather it shows us how to walk according to the map. Without the map, the compass is nearly useless. Without the compass, the map is worthless. The two together make a successful journey.

The Word of God is our map. Humility is our compass. Humility enables us to walk in the Word of God as the Holy Spirit reveals it to us. Francis Frangipane often speaks of humility as "the substructure of all change and transformation that takes place in our lives." The truth is that we cannot experience change until we are humble enough to admit the need for change. Until we see our need, there will never be reason to embrace the process that leads to change. You can't solve a problem without first acknowledging its existence.

We must also understand that where pride is present, grace is absent. The author of Proverbs recognized this truth:

When pride comes, then comes disgrace,
but with humility comes wisdom (Proverbs 11:2, NIV).

When pride takes up residence in a heart, grace leaves, but the infection remains. We are *dis-graced* when pride arrives. Grace departs and the filthy, darkened soil of pride is poured into the vacant garden of our hearts. In that soil, the seeds of covetousness, self-reliance, hatred, jealousy, lust, and so many other sins become planted. All of these forms of sin lead us downward toward destruction and will eventually bring forth their deadly fruit.

We need to understand humility if we are going to embrace the grace that is freely given to us by God. Humility brings grace and grace keeps us on the path of God's will. It enables us to overcome the temptation to jump on the fast track to the promise and bypass the character development we receive when we walk in God's will. It empowers us to change. The road to the promise, the divine detour, as we have learned, is all about change and only those who are humble can realize they need to change.

37

Know Thyself

Humility is honestly assessing ourselves in light of God's holiness and our sinfulness.

—C.J. Mahaney

I never truly understood humility until I read an intriguing verse in the Old Testament. During my devotional reading one day, I started to blaze through a verse of Scripture I hadn't noticed until the Holy Spirit stopped me in order to reveal the true meaning and definition of humility:

> *(Now Moses was very humble—more humble than any other person on earth) (Numbers 12:3, NLT).*

What makes this verse so interesting is who penned it. After I read it, I heard the voice of the Holy Spirit as me, "Who wrote this verse?"

Moses.

Think about that for a moment. How can anyone write a statement like that about himself? Of course, we have to remind ourselves that Moses wrote everything under the inspiration of the Holy Spirit, so he couldn't have written this in error. He didn't write this after a sudden burst of pride or to congratulate himself on attaining spiritual perfection. The Spirit of God directed him to write the truth.

And how was Moses able to write this if he was so humble?

"Simple," the Holy Spirit said to me that day. "He was able to write it because he *was* the most humble person in the world at the time!"

Therein lies the key to understanding the true nature of humility. Humility is knowing exactly who we are—gifts, flaws, strengths, weaknesses, capabilities, inabilities, successes, sins, assets, warts, and everything.

Humility is knowing exactly who we are.

Charles Spurgeon wrote, "Humility is to make a right estimate of one's self" (Spurgeon, 1869, 39). Paul was able to say it like this:

By the grace of God I am what I am, and His grace toward me did not prove vain; . . . (1 Corinthians 15:10, NASB).

To be completely honest, if I had written that verse, I would have said, "By the grace of God—*and with a lot of effort and striving and pushing and kicking and climbing ladders and keeping others down*—I am what I am." That's why it's a good thing God chose Paul to write it . . . because Paul recognized the true source of his identity and strength. He accepted his failings as opportunities for God's power to enter his life, and he accepted each strength as an undeserved gift of grace. Paul knew exactly who God created him to be.

The book of Revelation calls Satan "the accuser" (Revelation 12:10). He not only brings accusations against us before God, but he also tries to convince us we aren't who God made us to be. He started with a lie in the Garden of Eden. He said, in effect, "Eve, if you eat that fruit, you're going to find out who you really are. God doesn't want you to know how much like God you are, but if you eat the forbidden fruit, you're going to know good and evil just like God." Satan caused Eve to question her *identity*. He planted a seed of *insecurity* in the pride of her heart that sprouted to become fully developed rebellion.

Satan has since used this tactic repeatedly. Both kings and beggars have fallen to his deceptive strategies. He convinces the talented that they are their gift. He convinces them that they must get their identity from their gifts and the things they produce. And when their gift doesn't deliver, rejection sets in and insecurities arise. Billy Graham once said, "You are never more like the Devil than when you think you are your gift." That thinking was Lucifer's demise, and it's also our undoing if we give in to this temptation.

I believe Satan's primary objective in destroying the destiny of someone's life is to make the child of God question and doubt his or her true identity. This was his main tactic when he confronted Jesus and tempted Him in the wilderness. When John baptized Jesus in the Jordan River, the Spirit of God descended like a dove and a voice from heaven said, "This is my beloved Son, with whom I am well pleased" (Matthew 3:17, NIV). *Identity.*

The Spirit of God spoke exactly the words Jesus needed to hear. He had spent thirty years waiting, thirty years preparing for a three-year ministry.

No miracles.

No healings.

No sermons.

Just obedient obscurity.

God broke through the silence and confirmed the *identity* of His Son.

After that powerful, affirming experience, Jesus was immediately led by the Spirit into the wilderness for forty days, where He was tempted by the devil. The first thing the devil said was

"If you are the Son of God." He challenged Jesus' *identity.* Two of
the three recorded temptations were preceded by this conditional
statement—"If you are . . ." Satan knew that if he could get Jesus to
question His own identity Satan would have found an opportunity,
an open door to plant rebellion in Jesus. Satan needed to find the
soil of pride in Jesus' heart to plant his poisonous seed.

However, look at Jesus' answer to every one of the devil's
attempts to do so: "It is written." Jesus' identity was not wrapped up
in His gifting or His calling. It was defined by the Word of God.

> Jesus' identity was not wrapped
> up in His gifting or His calling.
> It was defined by the Word of God.

True humility is having a truthful estimate of yourself. Because
Jesus knew who He was, He was the most humble person ever to
walk the planet. He was secure.

Why is security so important? Because *not* knowing who you
really are, who God made you to be, is the source of personal
insecurity—pride. Insecure people make poor leaders because they
can't admit their need for help, accept responsibility for mistakes,
show weakness, or allow others to shine brighter than themselves.
Insecure people must always be the smartest, best, most capable
people in the room, and so they attempt to make others appear
smaller. They'll even go so far as to make others feel insecure in
order to maintain their superiority.

Insecurity is the leading indicator of pride. It's the cardinal sign and symptom that pride is present in a person's heart.
When taking pathology classes in pharmacy school, I had to
memorize the cardinal signs and symptoms of diseases. These
signs and symptoms are all *flags* pointing to something insidious and hidden to the casual observer. By learning the primary

flags of a particular disease, we can properly diagnose and treat the infirmity. Insecurity is a *flag* that waves in a person who has pride—*always*.

How can proud people be insecure when they seem to think so highly of themselves? Because proud people have the wrong estimate of themselves. Pride is to have the wrong estimate of one's self. Prideful people think they're something that they're not. They have an image of who they would like to be, so they create an environment around themselves that protects and upholds that image. Anyone who threatens that image is quickly dismissed or destroyed. Insecure people don't have security in the image they've created. Therefore, they fight to keep that image, even if it means hurting others in the process.

Pride is to have the wrong estimate of one's self.

True humility allows us to see ourselves for who we really are. With proper perspective, we can use God as the measure of greatness, instead of comparing ourselves to other people. When we look at Christ as our example, we see our spiritual growth for what it is. How can we view Him and the cross He bore without seeing the humility of the Lamb of God? Someone once asked Carl Henry how he could remain so humble while being so mightily used of God. He answered, "How can anyone be arrogant when he stands beside the cross?" (Mahaney, 2008, 606–607).

A few years ago, my wife and I experienced a series of extraordinary challenges and we were struggling to cope. We were bearing a cross. In the midst of it, we were lying in bed one evening, exhausted and bewildered, reflecting on the previous months. We talked about how, when we were teenagers together, we had all these visions of what ministry was going to be like and who we were going to be in our forties. We thought we were going to be strong and vibrant, a great man and woman of God. We thought we'd be spiritual giants, walking in such victory that people would almost be healed by our shadows.

I think many people can identify with our conversation. A lot of us thought we got a jump-start on this life with Christ. Many, like my wife and I, got started in high school. We never thought we'd be lying in bed as a forty-something, thinking, "How did we get here?" The closer I grew to God and the more I knew of His truth, the more I became aware of my own failures. As I grew, I learned more, I prayed more, I gave more, yet I didn't feel more spiritually developed than the year before. Why was this so? Because I became increasingly aware of just how powerless I was without Christ. I was getting to know who I really am.

I don't suffer from an overactive conscience, and I don't have a superiority complex. In fact, I find myself in good company with Paul, who wrote:

> For I am the least of the apostles and do not even deserve to be called an apostle, because I persecuted the church of God (1 Corinthians 15:9, NIV).

While Paul was one of the greatest followers of Christ ever to live, he recognized his daily need for the grace of God. Several years later, in a letter to the church at Ephesus, Paul referred to himself as "the very least of all saints" (Ephesians 3:8). Near the end of his life, Paul wrote to Timothy, his son in the faith:

> . . . Christ Jesus came into the world to save sinners, among whom I am foremost of all. Yet for this reason I found mercy, so that in me as the foremost, Jesus Christ might demonstrate His perfect patience as an example for those who would believe in Him for eternal life (1 Timothy 1:15–16, NASB).

I see a clear progression in Paul's life, from "least of apostles," then "least of saints," and finally, "the foremost of sinners." Paul's example convinces me that the more Christlike our character becomes, the further from His likeness we *feel*. The closer, more accurate glimpse we have of God and His revealed holiness and glory, the more we see ourselves as we really are. John Calvin once wrote, "It is evident that man never attains to a true self-knowledge until he has previously contemplated the face of God, and come down after such contemplation to look into himself" (Calvin, 1990, 38). When we see God as He is, we are actually developing the right estimate of ourselves. This true estimate is the essence of humility. It lies in direct opposition to insecurity.

I find that the closer I grow in my relationship with the Lord, the more I realize that nothing in the journey, nor the promise, is about my glory. It is all about *His* glory. The pathway of His divine detour will become clearer as humility is cultivated in our hearts. As God cultivates in us a humble spirit, often in our wilderness places, we more readily accept that our lives, dreams, and promises have very little to do with us and our glory. It's all about *Him* and *His* glory. As that truth settles into the hidden recesses of our hearts, the less important our will and our way become in the grand design of God's journey with us. With an understanding of the beauty of humility, we learn that it is the virtue of all virtues, and the essence of all that is good.

38

Root or Fruit?

Humility is a great and most essential thing in true religion. The whole frame of the gospel, and everything appertaining to the new covenant, and all dispositions towards fallen man, are calculated to bring to pass this effect [humility] in the hearts of men. They that are destitute of this, have not true religion, whatever profession they make, and how high soever their religious affections may be.

—Jonathan Edwards

Humility is important.

I believe we don't have a grace problem in the church. I believe we have a humility problem. Humility, as I mentioned previously, is the prerequisite of grace. Humility brings grace. So why is humility the least talked about, most avoided subject in our churches today?

William Law (1686–1761) made this observation of his generation, but it applies to ours as well: "Generally speaking, it [humility] is the least understood, the least regarded, the least intended, the least desired and sought after, of all other virtues, amongst all sorts of Christians." It is not a popular subject.

I would estimate that I have heard, at the most, two messages dedicated entirely to the subject of humility. Sadly, I don't even remember them as something inspiring. Churches teach about love, blessing, worship, joy, peace, and the list goes on. But no one wants to talk about the root of it all—humility.

Humility is not a fruit of the Spirit. Humility is the root of the Spirit. It is the soil in which the fruit of the Spirit grows.

Humility is not a fruit of the Spirit. Humility is the root of the Spirit.

You can't love without humility. You can't have peace without humility. You can't have self-control without humility. Humility is the virtue of all virtues. Andrew Murray says it this way:

> Humility is the only soil in which the virtues of grace may grow: the lack of humility is the sufficient explanation of every defect and failure. Humility is not so much a grace or virtue along with others; it is the root of all, because it alone takes the right attitude before God, and allows Him as God to do all.

Humility is a posture of the heart. It takes, as Murray says, the right attitude before God. As we discussed earlier, humility is how you know who you are. When you know yourself, then you will know who God is and what your position is before Him.

William P. Farley provides this observation when he says:

> Since humility ends in trembling at God's Word, it brings us into real communion with God. It sensitizes us to God's voice. It opens our ears to his instructions. It amplifies gratitude. It intensifies dependence. In other words, the humble see their need for God.

Walking in the will of God does just what Farley describes; it "intensifies" our dependence in Him. We know we need God.

That is the beauty of divine detours. They create opportunities for humble activities.

God created the world out of nothing, and as long as we are nothing, He can make something out of us.

—*Martin Luther*

39

An Unavoidable Choice

Far from offering us flattery, the cross undermines our self-righteousness, and we can stand before it only with a bowed head and a broken spirit.

—*John Stott*

On your divine detour, you will find endless opportunities to display the Christlike virtue of humility. Remember these words from Deuteronomy?

Remember how the Lord your God led you all the way in the wilderness these forty years, to humble and test you in order to know what was in your heart, whether or not you would keep his commands (Deuteronomy 8:2, NIV).

God designed the detour with humility in mind. Detours do not actually create humility in us; they only give us opportunities to develop it. Detours reveal the areas of pride still residing in our hearts so that we can address them. The next verse in Deuteronomy describes this process:

He humbled you, causing you to hunger and then feeding you with manna, which neither you nor your ancestors had known, to teach you that man does not live on bread alone but on every word that comes from the mouth of the Lord (Deuteronomy 8:3, NIV).

Pride is dependent on self for provision and supply. Humility, on the other hand, is just the opposite. It is characterized by our dependency on God. Humility is our choice to make God our provision and supply. Andrew Murray said, "Humility is the displacement of self by the enthronement of God. Where God is all, self is nothing" (Murray, 2012, 31).

> Detours do not actually create humility in us; they only give us opportunities to develop it.

Throughout Scripture, God issues multiple orders for us to humble ourselves. Humility is a choice *we* make. No one, including God, can create humility in us. Sure, He can certainly create opportunities for humility to be formed, but the choice is always ours to make. In fact, I call it an *unavoidable choice*. That may sound like an oxymoron, but the truth is we are *all* humbled. The only question is, *how* will we be humbled?

And whosoever shall fall on this stone shall be broken: but on whomsoever it shall fall, it will grind him to powder (Matthew 21:44, KJV).

> . . . the truth is we are *all* humbled. The only question is, *how* will we be humbled?

In this verse, Jesus was speaking to a crowd of prideful, religious leaders. The Greek word used here for *broken* means, "to break into small pieces." The word used for *powder* means, "powder." Do you see the difference? You can chose one or the other. Either fall on the Rock, Jesus, and be broken. Or wait for the Rock to fall on you and be ground to powder. I think I'll choose to fall on the Rock. Brokenness is not necessarily something I normally choose, but it certainly sounds better than the alternative—powder! Will you humble yourself or be humbled? The choice really is yours to make.

One of the main objections people often have to humility is the idea that humility is a sign of weakness. Likewise, some people view brokenness from a standpoint of not functioning properly or needing to be fixed. But with God, brokenness is a thing of beauty. The Psalmist declares:

> *The sacrifices of God are a broken spirit,*
> *A broken and a contrite heart—*
> *These, O God, You will not despise (Psalm 51:17, NKJV).*

Brokenness attracts God. It is the sacrifice He loves. True brokenness cannot be faked. You can see it evident in a person.

During my early years of ministry, a guest speaker came to the church where I served. He was a precious man who had left the U.S. years before and dedicated his life to serving the underground church in China. After the service, I had the privilege of taking him to dinner. I remember sitting across the table from him and telling him all the marvelous things God was doing through our church and through my ministry. Meanwhile, he kindly smiled and continued to eat. After I finished telling him how wonderful I was, he asked me a question, "Sion, what do you know about brokenness?" The question rather caught me off guard, but I muttered, "Why, it's important, of course." Looking past all of my pride, he looked into my eyes and told me something I will never forget. He said, "Sion, God desires brokenness in you. One day, if you are truly submitted to Him, you will understand the beauty of brokenness."

Honestly, at the time, I thought the man totally missed it with me. I thought I was broken. After all, I had left a lucrative job in pharmacy to be a full-time minister of this church. I had sacrificed, I'd given up a lot in order to follow God. Brokenness, I thought, was a given. However, God wasn't interested in my sacrifices; He was interested in my brokenness.

God uses broken vessels. Vessels who walk with a limp. Vessels who understand that any good thing that flows out of them is not from them. Broken vessels don't take the credit or ask for the seat of honor. They seek the lowest position in every room.

> God uses broken vessels.
> Vessels who walk with a limp.

Years later, I learned that only the broken can see the broken. It takes a broken person to recognize someone who is truly broken. And it is beautiful. Brokenness enables us to recognize our weaknesses. Moreover, these weaknesses are not our enemy; they are opportunities for His power.

40

The Strength of Weakness

At journey's end, the proud will still be dithering around deluded;
but the humble will have forged a special freedom, for they have
forgotten about themselves entirely.
— *Thomas A. Jones*

Humbling experiences along the pathway of God's divine detours inevitably lead to seasons of extraordinary spiritual growth. What we go through determines what we become based on *how* we go through it. As I stated earlier, going through difficulties doesn't make you stronger; it's *how* you go through difficulties that will determine your strength.

There is a great paradox on the journey to God's promise. Hidden pride often feels like strength, while humility feels like weakness. In a world where people are always striving for a place of importance, we think of weakness as a bad thing when, in fact, God says we are never stronger than when we are weak. The Bible reveals that our weakness and brokenness actually open the way for God's power and strength.

> The Bible reveals that our weakness
> and brokenness actually open the
> way for God's power and strength.

The apostle Paul described how God works in his second letter to the believers at Corinth. The Corinthians continually struggled with an overblown estimation of their own importance. To help them see how God used him so powerfully, Paul shared a very personal struggle:

> ... Therefore, in order to keep me from becoming conceited, I was given a thorn in my flesh, a messenger of Satan, to torment me. Three times I pleaded with the Lord to take it away from me. But he said to me, "My grace is sufficient for you, for my power is made perfect in weakness." Therefore I will boast all the more gladly about my weaknesses, so that Christ's power may rest on me. That is why, for Christ's sake, I delight in weaknesses, in insults, in hardships, in persecutions, in difficulties. For when I am weak, then I am strong (2 Corinthians 12:7–10, NIV).

Look closely at the Lord's reassurance to Paul. While he asked God to deliver him from Satan's affliction, God assured His servant Paul that the allowed affliction had a purpose. God didn't cause Paul's suffering; Satan caused it. But the Lord gave Paul's suffering a divine purpose. He allowed the hardship to remain so Paul wouldn't become conceited, and to make His power (*dunamis*) perfect in the apostle's life.

Paul never identifies his thorn, because the specific issue is irrelevant. It could have been a physical ailment, a relentless enemy, a particular temptation, an emotional or psychological problem, or a recurring illness. He didn't focus on his issue; he helped his readers identify with his experience as we think about our own thorns.

We do know the affliction irritated his flesh and tormented him. But God didn't remove the source of Paul's weakness. Instead, God left the thorn to remind Paul of his inability to do anything outside the grace of God. The thorn served as a reminder that, despite great revelations, Paul was still a man.

This experience kept the apostle dependent upon God for strength, which made him far more effective in fulfilling God's purpose for his life.

Weakness. That's not a popular word in most self-help books. You won't hear motivational speakers talk about weakness as a means to become great. No one lists "weakness" as a dominant trait or area of strength on a resume. While many leadership experts urge others to empower themselves, they teach strategies to overcome weakness. Even so, Paul calls us to embrace the thorns that reveal and disclose our weaknesses. According to Paul, weakness is a prerequisite to strength.

Note that God's power is *made perfect* in weakness. The Greek term used for perfect here is *teleos*, and it carries the idea of process with purpose. *Teleos* moves toward a specific, defined, predetermined outcome. It's less about being without flaw and more about becoming all God created you to be. God uses our weakness as a means of accomplishing in us what He ultimately desires—Christlike character.

With all of this in mind, here's what I consider a biblical definition of weakness: "Our inability to obey God in our own strength or by our own ability." We cannot obey God's moral commands without His divine help (grace), and we are incapable of doing His work apart from His supernatural power.

> … here's what I consider a biblical definition of weakness: "Our inability to obey God in our own strength or by our own ability."

What do you consider your greatest weakness? What do you feel powerless to overcome? What "thorn" have you repeatedly asked God to remove, yet still it remains in your flesh? Have you considered that God may want you to accept your thorn? Have you considered how God might channel His power through your weakness? Have you admitted your inability to do anything about this affliction? Can you say with Paul, "For Christ's sake, I delight in weaknesses, in insults, in hardships, in persecutions, in difficulties. For when I am weak, then I am strong" (2 Corinthians 12:10, NIV)? If so, you can be sure that His power is being made perfect in you.

We often hear the last part of Paul's discourse misquoted, "When I am weak, He is strong." But Paul actually declared, "When I am weak, *I* am strong." When I am in a place where I put no confidence in my own strength, in my own gifting, or in my own wisdom, then I am really strong, because His power is made perfect (complete and lacking nothing) in my weakness.

Paul was talking about a weakness of the human soul to obey the will and Word of God. We can't do it without His power. We can't walk in God's will without His grace. We *need* Him. We are dependent on Him. This is a true act of humility—an attitude of total dependence on His ability. Andrew Murray said, "Learn to be nothing, learn to be helpless. The man who has got something is not absolutely dependent; but the man who has got nothing is absolutely dependent. Absolute dependence upon God is the secret of all power in work" (Murray, 2011, 2487–2489).

Once we arrive at this conclusion after embracing our thorn, God's promise is that He will give us His grace. He says:

". . . My grace is sufficient for you . . ." (2 Corinthians 12:9, NIV).

The word sufficient used in this text is *arkeo*, which means "to aid, assist, to be strong enough" (Vine, Unger, and White, 1996). His grace is enough! It is all you need. If you've prayed three times as Paul did and your situation hasn't changed, embrace the thorn. Welcome to His divine detour. His grace will be there to aid you, assist you, and give you strength. Then you will be strong!

41

Learning to Be Teachable

One of the great lessons of the journey is the lesson of learning to be a learner. Being teachable is an indicator that you are humble because only through humility do we demonstrate that we are willing to learn. Winston Churchill said it well: "I am always ready to learn although I do not always like being taught." I think that's the way it is with all of us while we're on the divine detour. We understand the importance of learning, but don't necessarily enjoy the position of a student. It is a humble position.

Look again at God's instruction in Deuteronomy:

He humbled you, causing you to hunger and then feeding you with manna, which neither you nor your ancestors had known, to teach you that man does not live on bread alone but on every word that comes from the mouth of the Lord (Deuteronomy 8:3, NIV).

God humbles us by allowing the circumstance we're in to turn us into willing students. Being teachable is a lesson of the wilderness. In the case of the people of Israel, their hunger became a powerful motivator. God satisfied the people's hunger with manna that fell from heaven every morning, six days a week. This was a lesson for both Israel as well as us, so we would understand that we must live off of every word proceeding from the mouth of God. King Solomon wrote:

> *The fear of the Lord is the beginning of knowledge;*
> *fools despise wisdom and instruction (Proverbs 1:7, ESV).*

Humility opens our minds to learning. Being humble is being teachable. As the great sage of the basketball court, John Wooden, once said, "It's what you learn *after* you know it all that counts." Humility is behind all change that takes place in our lives, and this includes gaining wisdom. If you want to learn and grow, you must admit your need for learning.

This truth doesn't only apply to intellectual development; it applies to *all* areas of life. In the same way a student must submit to the lessons of a teacher, a humble spirit submits to the instruction of the Holy Spirit, who uses all aspects of life to transform our minds. Consequently, a humble spirit remains open to correction and instruction regardless of the source.

On the other hand, prideful people remain unteachable. They surround themselves with people who won't tell them the truth. They seek people who will agree with them to stroke their delicate egos. They attract pliable, emotionally needy people who are too weak to speak the truth. Unfortunately, I see too many powerful leaders receive flattery after doing something stupid or wrong.

Several years ago, our staff at Gateway Church took Gallup's *StrengthsFinder* test to determine our top five leadership strengths. We did this exercise so that we could understand each other and function better as a team. It was a tremendous help. One of the strengths that showed up in my top five was "learner." This wasn't a surprise to me. I *love* to learn. I tend to get a little obsessive-compulsive about things and want to learn everything I can about them. I read magazines, website forums, and books about any subject I'm interested in until I know quite a bit about the topic. For some reason, I get enjoyment out of it. But even though I have this strength, I've come to realize that learning isn't the same as being teachable. Learners don't have to be humble to learn, but they do have to be humble to be teachable.

John Maxwell explains being teachable by saying, "A man must be big enough to admit his mistakes, smart enough to profit from them, and strong enough to correct them." If learning was a sign of humility, then the great institutions of learning would be filled with humble people. Learning doesn't make you humble. If anything, the Word of God tells us that ". . . knowledge puffs us up" (1 Corinthians 8:1). Being teachable is more about positioning ourselves in a place where we submit our ideas and our will to the teacher. We allow the teacher to correct and adjust our thinking. Learning is only the act of accumulating information. Being teachable is an act of submission.

Learning is only the act of accumulating
information. Being teachable
is an act of submission.

42

The Great Protector of Humility

"We must totally disagree when we hear that the president of the National Organization of Women declares that 'submission to another human being is always wrong.' However, we must never forget that ultimately we are to submit to God, and that submission to men must always fit within God's will—or else we cannot obey" (*Jones and Fontenot, 2012, 65*).

When teaching on pride in classrooms and at conferences, I always get asked during the Q&A portions about how we can protect ourselves against pride. The simple answer is *submission*. The truth is, *everyone* needs accountability. All of us need people who love us enough to say, "Listen, friend, you shouldn't have said that (or done that.) It was wrong." We need people in our lives who will be real with us. We need people who will step up and be honest about their observations. We need people who aren't afraid of us. And in order to keep those people close, we must humble ourselves. When it comes to churches, businesses, and ministries, we must cultivate an environment of mutual submission, where subordinates in our organization complete the tasks assigned to them, yet they feel completely at ease telling us the truth. Because, let's face it, if someone relies on you for a paycheck, and doesn't feel secure in the position, you will never hear anything but good news and happy lies.

An open, accountable environment of mutual submission won't happen automatically. In fact, we can destroy it rather innocently and unintentionally. Years ago, I was a youth pastor and had been in prayer about a fantastic idea for our youth ministry. I was so excited about it. I felt like God had given me a great plan to reach the young people in our community. The next day I prepared a proposal to take to my pastor. I planned it down to the last detail. In fact, I prepared two proposals—the one I really wanted with its actual cost and another one with an inflated cost that I knew he would reject. I knew him well and had learned how to get what I wanted. So, I went into his office, sat down, and said, "Pastor, God gave me this incredible plan . . ."

Right there and then, God convicted me. A little voice inside my head said, "*Sion, you're being manipulative.*" If you ever go to anyone and say, "God told me," you've already trumped their authority by claiming a divine mandate. You've just overridden any good thing they might have to say. In that case, you're not submitting, you're manipulating. It's better to go to your authority and say, "I was in prayer and I'm *feeling* something." You take that thing you're considering and submit it to your authority and your peers for checks and balances. You explain your idea to those who report to you and encourage their honest feedback. But do not pull the "God card." Always leave the door open for your authority to speak the Lord's wisdom into the situation.

In spite of my attempt to manipulate, my pastor did exactly that—he spoke wisdom into the situation. In response to my "God gave this idea to me" statement, he said, "This seems like a great idea. I just don't think the timing is right for such an endeavor. Keep all this information, and when the time is right, we can make a decision then about whether to do this or not." He overruled me, but I learned a valuable lesson. My unchecked pride had led me to manipulate my leader.

Months later, I looked back and realized my idea wouldn't have worked. We would have wasted money and time. I think God let me do that to teach me a lesson. He wanted me to go into that office and submit my beloved idea to my pastor, and He wanted me to remain open to honest feedback. That would have been true submission.

Prideful people love to criticize their boss. They always know better than the people God has placed in authority over them. And, let's be honest, many times the boss does know less than the people the boss leads. Even so, God says:

> *Obey your leaders and submit to them, for they are keeping watch over your souls, as those who will have to give an account. Let them do this with joy and not with groaning, for that would be of no advantage to you (Hebrews 13:17, ESV).*

God didn't say, "Obey your leaders if you agree with them." No, God says to obey and submit. Not simply obey. Not merely submit. But both obey *and* submit.

Although they may seem like the same thing, there is a difference between obedience and submission. Obedience deals with your *actions*, while submission deals with your *attitude*. In the case of my grand plan, I ended up obeying my pastor. But I wasn't submitted. My attitude was, "He can't hear from God like I can. He doesn't know. He'll find out the hard way."

Obedience deals with your *actions*,
while submission deals with your *attitude*.

If you have kids, you know what I mean, especially if they're teenagers. When I tell one of my kids, "Go clean up your room." They turn to obey, but I sometimes sense them rolling their eyes. They may have obeyed, but their heart didn't honor their father. There was no submission. Long ago, my wife and I realized God was calling us to discipline our children's attitudes and not just their actions, because God has instructed all of us to *submit* to authority and not just *obey* it.

Submission to authority is an important subject. I believe the greater the calling, the higher the platform of influence and the greater the gifting, the more submission needs to have its place in our lives. Submission is proof of humility. And it is also the great protector of humility. You will never get to a place in life where you don't need true submission.

> Submission is proof of humility. And it
> is also the great protector of humility.

My dear friend and authority at Gateway Church, Thomas Miller, says it like this, "You can't truly walk in authority until you are submitted to authority." When God promotes you to a position in His kingdom, it is always to a place of authority. He doesn't, however, promote you to a place that no longer requires submission. That truth goes for business owners, pastors, politicians, and everyone else. No one is to live without the covering of authority. We are all called to submit ourselves to one another, as Paul says, "Submit to one another out of reverence for Christ" (Ephesians 5:21, NIV).

But you may say, "Sion, I *would* submit to my authority, but they just don't understand me and they're holding me back from my calling." Let me comfort you with these words: There is no authority that God has not established, including the one you are talking about:

> *Let everyone be subject to the governing authorities, for*
> *there is no authority except that which God has established.*

The authorities that exist have been established by God. Consequently, whoever rebels against the authority is rebelling against what God has instituted, and those who do so will bring judgment on themselves (Romans 13:1–2, NIV).

Again. There is *no* authority except that which God has established. As bad as this sounds, it is also comforting. The reason you are placed under the authority in your life is because God knows you will grow there. I understand that's hard to accept, but it is true!

Nearly every month, I get a phone call from a worship pastor who feels like God is calling him or her to another church because the pastor and leadership of their church don't see the potential and giftings in them. They've hit a ceiling and want out. But let me tell you what I tell them: God knows the perfect environment where your gift needs to be planted. He knows what you need, and He has planted you there for one purpose—*to change you.*

God never places you in a position so you can change those in authority over you. He places you there to change *you.* You are not sent to a church to change the pastor. You are not sent to a business to change the boss. You are not sent to a school to change its teachers. And you are not in your marriage to change your spouse. You are where God has placed you because He wants to change *you.*

God never places you in a position so you can change those in authority over you. He places you there to change *you.*

That is the blessing of submission. We are changed when we are submitted. God uses our authorities to reveal our unholy motives. Submission is humbling. Submission is the key to fulfilling the call of God on your life. We have been discussing the journey and how God uses divine detours to create Christlikeness in us. Out of all the lessons, the hardest and most valuable may be the lesson of submission.

A great, gifted stallion may be powerful and beautiful as it roams free in the wild. The master may capture it and keep it within the confines of the ranch, but until the horse is broken, it is of no use to the master. Though majestic and captivating, the full potential of the horse will never be realized until it is submitted. *Submission is not a sign of strength weakened; submission is power under authority.* Until the bit and bridle have made their way into the mouth of the stallion, all the power and glory of the animal is lost in selfish rebellion.

Submission is not a sign of strength weakened; submission is power under authority.

We will never reach our full potential if we don't understand submission. Our callings, our gifts, and ultimately our hearts must be submitted to God's earthly, established authority or we will never achieve the dream and promise He has for us.

43

Put It On

Jesus Christ took the place and fulfilled the destiny of man, as a creature, by his life of perfect humility. His humility is our salvation. His salvation is our humility.

—*Andrew Murray*

If our goal is to embrace the mantle of humility, we need to look no further than Jesus Himself for instruction and inspiration on how to obtain this virtue. His words are simple: "*. . . learn from me, for I am gentle and humble in heart . . .*" (Matthew 11:29, NIV). Jesus is the greatest example of humility to grace the face of the earth. He is greater than Moses, greater than Paul, and even greater than John the Baptist of whom Jesus spoke when He said:

". . . Truly I tell you, among those born of women there has not risen anyone greater than John the Baptist; yet whoever is least in the kingdom of heaven is greater than he" (Matthew 11:11, NIV).

We are to learn from Him. If we desire to live in Him, we are to walk as He walked:

Whoever claims to live in him must live as Jesus did (1 John 2:6, NIV).

The incredible thing about Jesus' humility is that it was His choice. He *chose* to walk in humility. When Paul wrote to the church in Philippi, he said we should have the same attitude Christ had when He made the choice to humble Himself:

> *Let this same attitude* and *purpose* and *[humble] mind be in you which was in Christ Jesus: [Let Him be your example in humility:]*
>
> *Who, although being essentially one with God* and *in the form of God [possessing the fullness of the attributes which make God God], did not think this equality with God was a thing to be eagerly grasped* or *retained,*
>
> *but stripped Himself [of all privileges and rightful dignity], so as to assume the guise of a servant (slave), in that He became like men* and *was born a human being.*
>
> *And after He had appeared in human form, He abased* and *humbled Himself [still further] and carried His obedience to the extreme of death, even the death of the cross!*
>
> *Therefore [because He stooped so low] God has highly exalted Him and has freely bestowed on Him the name that is above every name (Philippians 2:5–9, Amplified Bible, Classic Edition).*

This is our example. This is who we learn from. Jesus Himself. He stripped Himself of all the privileges and rights that come with being the Son of God and assumed the position of a servant. He became like us, mere flesh and blood, and was born a human. He then went further and obeyed His Father, even when it meant He would have to die a criminal's death on a cross.

It was His choice to embrace the lowliness of humanity that gave His humility its power. He wasn't forced to do it, He *chose* to do it. Therefore, it was His humility that gave His death its value. Had he been forced, His death wouldn't have anywhere near the same value. Humility gave Christ's death its value.

Humility gave Christ's death its value.

Is it ironic that pride was the cause of humanity's demise and humility its resurrection? I don't think so. I think it was orchestrated by God. It was in His divine plan all along. Pride brought death into the world, but humility brought life. No wonder the greatest battlefield of the mind is that of pride versus humility.

So what are we to do? How are we to walk with humility? The answer is to *put it on*. Humility isn't something we pray for and receive at an altar. We have to *put it on*. It requires action on our part:

> *In the same way, you who are younger must accept the authority of the elders. And all of you, dress yourselves in humility as you relate to one another, for*
>
> *"God opposes the proud*
> *but gives grace to the humble."*
>
> *So humble yourselves under the mighty power of God, and at the right time he will lift you up in honor* (1 Peter 5:5–6, NLT).

We must purposely *put on* humility, because it doesn't come naturally to us.

Every morning, before leaving home, you get dressed. You pick out your clothes, coordinate them by style and color, and then put them on. Clothes are not a natural part of our bodies. Not one of us came into this world wearing clothes. Unfortunately, we weren't born with humility either. We have to put on humility just as must we put on clothes.

We also have to remember that we must clothe ourselves *daily*. Putting on humility isn't a one-time event; it's a lifestyle. Yesterday's clothes don't smell good today. They must be replaced. Changing clothes needs to be a regular part of our routine. Before we step onto a platform, before we walk into that meeting, before our spouse comes home from a hard day at work, and before we go home to our spouse from a hard day at work, we have to *put it on*. Clothe yourself with humility, the state of mind and attitude that Jesus had.

> ## Putting on humility isn't a one-time event; it's a lifestyle.

Finally, we obey the will of God even when it leads to our own death. Because that is where humility ultimately leads—*self-death*. God may not ask us to offer up our lives in one grand, selfless gesture. More often, He asks us to surrender our lives in daily increments when we set aside our desires in favor of those we serve. This is the way of the cross. This is what walking in the Spirit is all about. This is true worship:

> *Therefore, I urge you, brothers and sisters, in view of God's mercy, to offer your bodies as a living sacrifice, holy and pleasing to God—this is your true and proper worship. Do not conform to the pattern of this world, but be transformed by the renewing of your mind. Then you will be able to test and approve what God's will is—his good, pleasing and perfect will* (Romans 12:1–2, NIV).

Once we walk in a place of surrender, humility, and obedience, we will be able to "test and approve what God's will is."

Did you catch that?

We can know His good, pleasing and perfect will!

We can come to the place where we *understand* and *recognize* we are on a *divine detour!*

This walk of humility is a walk of worship patterned after the steps of Jesus Himself. His obedient walk led Him to a cross and so will ours—a cross that kills everything that's not of God so nothing remains but His resurrection power. And the more we walk the path, the more we will understand His will, until one day we wake up and find ourselves right in the middle of the promise!

44

The Reward

*Success is a journey, not a destination. The doing is often more
important than the outcome.*

—*Arthur Ashe*

In 2006, just after the Pittsburgh Steelers won the Super Bowl,
I read an article on the sporting news website in which the head
coach, Bill Cowher, reflected on the aftermath of his team's victory.
Part of the celebration honors included a visit to the White House
to meet the President. As Cowher walked into the East Room, he
noticed rows of Velcro strips lining the floor where aides placed
nametags for each player. He immediately noticed his name had
been spelled "Cower" instead of "Cowher."

Some people would have been upset, but the coach shrugged
it off. "You know," he said, "being in the White House really put
everything into perspective. All we do is throw this little ball down
the field and run from one end to the other. The man we were
about to meet is tackling problems much bigger than football.
The Super Bowl win actually taught me humility," he said. "It's not
about winning the championship. It was about the process in getting there. I actually cherish the journey more than I do the trophy."

You know the journey, the divine detour, has done its job when
you can stand at the finish line and say in your heart, "I would

rather have the experiences of the journey than the vanity of the trophy." Why? Because the journey gives you something. The journey is where God's character is developed in you. The journey is where you are trained. The journey is where you are tried and tested. The journey changes your perspective. The promise may have been the goal at the beginning of the journey, but now it's an afterthought compared to the rich treasures we uncovered on the diving detour.

> You know the journey, the divine detour,
> has done its job when you can stand at
> the finish line and say in your heart,
> "I would rather have the experiences of the
> journey than the vanity of the trophy."

I have reached the promise in many areas of my life. Some big ones. Some smaller. I reached them God's way, by submitting myself to the process. Suffering. Waiting. Changing. Suffering. Waiting. Changing. Some divine detours lasted a decade. Some lasted a day. But they all had one purpose. They all had one goal—*Christlikeness*.

I have also taken some shortcuts—fast tracks to the promise. I chased my dreams. I pursued my vision. I bypassed processes and left the paths of His will in search of easier travel. Prideful. Arrogant. Conceited. "I did it my way," I sang as I crossed the finish line. Those journeys I regret. The people I hurt, the bridges I burned, and the relationships I sacrificed—only painful memories surround those victories. The dust on those trophies serves as a reminder that the process has a purpose, and I elected to forfeit the benefits.

God lured me into all of these journeys with a promise. A dream. A vision of something better than that with which I was familiar. And throughout the journey, my thoughts of these things inspired me to continue, no matter how hard or rough the road was. Hope was developed. Faith resulted. Mountains were moved. The finish line was crossed.

Each divine detour taught me something unique. But I'm not finished with detours. I'm on a half dozen or so as I write this. But let my limited experience in journey-walking be an encouragement to you, and let this next sentence sink down into your heart and never be forgotten.

The journey is the reward.

The divine detour, the process, the pain, the suffering, the trials, the test, the tribulations, and the waiting, these things are now the trophies I claim as valuable. Not the positions I may have added. Not the fame I may have gained. Not the money or noto-riety that often comes when promises are fulfilled. The journey *itself* is the prize.

The journey *itself* is the prize.

Reading that interview with Bill Cowher opened my eyes to something I was missing while traveling the road of God's will toward a distant promise. *I needed to enjoy the trip.* I needed the atti-tude and perspective of Christ when I walked through hardships. I needed to remember that wildernesses and deserts were designed for paths, not permanent settlements. The detours were not my destina-tion. I was only a pilgrim passing through. But I needed to embrace each thorn, each trial, each hardship, and each difficulty and know that character—Christlike character—was my destiny.

Today I feel like I am a better husband to my wonderful wife. I feel like I am a better father to my eight beautiful children. None of this happened because I achieved some dreams, or because I crossed some finish lines. It happened because I have a more

Christlike character. I know I haven't arrived, and I know I have more journeys to travel, but I walk them differently now. I've come to expect the divine detours.

Remember Joseph? Remember his dream? Remember how he saw his brothers all bowing down to him? Remember how excited he was when he told his father that everyone in the family, including Dad, would one day bow and serve him? Seventeen years later, Joseph had a different perspective of his God-given dream. The Scripture picks up the story sometime after Joseph's brothers have come to Egypt for assistance because of a great famine. When Joseph reveals himself to his brothers, they naturally think he's going to exact revenge on them for the cruelty they showed him. Instead, they encountered a much different brother than the one they threw in the pit. This one is humble. This one is compassionate and merciful. Listen to Joseph's interpretation of his dream now:

> *"And now, do not be distressed and do not be angry with yourselves for selling me here, because it was to save lives that God sent me ahead of you. For two years now there has been famine in the land, and for the next five years there will not be plowing and reaping. But God sent me ahead of you to preserve for you a remnant on earth and to save your lives by a great deliverance"* (Genesis 45:5–7, NIV; emphasis added).

Did you notice the object of his dream now? It wasn't himself; it was his family. It was his brothers and their families. All along, the dream wasn't about Joseph; it was about the "great deliverance" God had planned for His people. Joseph was simply the instrument of that redemptive work. Yes, Joseph's dream involved him using his gifts and talents. And yes, it took him to a high platform of influence, but it was not about Joseph; it was all about others.

Twice Joseph said, "God sent me ahead of you." There was no blame. There was no revenge. Only peaceful rejoicing that God's will had been done despite the evil that brought him low. All things worked together for the good.

Joseph was so at peace with the journey that he even gave his two sons names that signified his changed heart:

> *Joseph named his firstborn Manasseh and said, "It is because God has made me forget all my trouble and all my father's household." The second son he named Ephraim and said, "It is because God has made me fruitful in the land of my suffering"* (Genesis 41:51–52, NIV).

Joseph suffered successfully. He was better, not bitter, because of what he endured. He realized his dream and his gifts were about serving, not being served. Now, on the better side of the pit, Joseph understood that the gifts had been entrusted to him to serve his family. His heart had to be trained for this position. He needed the character to handle the platform. If he hadn't submitted to the process of God and allowed character to be developed in his heart while in the prison and in the pit, the power of the palace would have easily corrupted him. Revenge would have been his natural inclination when his brothers crawled to his feet. Instead, he was used as an instrument by God to bring a great deliverance to His people.

> Joseph suffered successfully. He was better,
> not bitter, because of what he endured.

That is the purpose of our gifts. Our gifts are given so we may serve others. As Peter said:

> *Each of you should use whatever gift you have received to serve others, as faithful stewards of God's grace in its various forms* (1 Peter 4:10, NIV).

Everyone has been given something to do that shows who God is (1 Corinthians 12:7). That is your gift. You are a conduit of God's glory for the entire world to experience.

Seek God—the Promise Giver. Submit to His will. Walk in His Spirit on the pathway to His promise. Don't take shortcuts. Be patient. Let character be developed inside you. Receive the promise when it comes and stand in your Promised Land rejoicing that the journey is the reward! Know that His divine detours were actually doorways to your dream!

> *I walked a mile with Pleasure*
> *She chattered all the way*
> *But left me none the wiser*
> *For all she had to say*
>
> *I walked a mile with Sorrow*
> *And ne'er a word said she*
> *But, oh, the things I learned from her*
> *When sorrow walked with me*

Author Unknown

Bibliography

Brand, Chad, Charles Draper, and Archie England. "Shekinah." In *Holman Illustrated Bible Dictionary*. Nashville, TN: Holman Bible Publishers, 2003.

Calvin, Jean. *Institutes of the Christian Religion*. Vol. 1. Grand Rapids, MI: Wm. B. Eerdmans, 1990.

Duffield, Guy P., and Van Cleave Nathaniel M. *Foundations of Pentecostal Theology*. Los Angeles, CA: Foursquare Media, 2008.

Kaiser, Walter C. "Exodus." Edited by Frank E. Gaebelein. In *The Expositor's Bible Commentary: With the New International Version of the Holy Bible*. Grand Rapids, MI: Zondervan, 1992.

Giglio, Louie. *Worship: That Thing We Do*. Passion Conference. Atlanta: 268 Generation, 2012. DVD.

Gorman, Mark. Sermon, 2014.

Hayford, Jack W. *The Reward of Worship: The Joy of Fellowship with a Personal God*. Grand Rapids, MI: Chosen Books, 2007.

Jones, Thomas A., and Michael Fontenot. *The Prideful Soul's Guide to Humilty*. Billerica, MA: Discipleship Publications International, 2003. Kindle.

Keil, Carl Friedrich, and Franz Delitzsch. *Commentary on the Old Testament*. Peabody, MA: Hendrickson, 1996.

Kielburger, Marc. "Faculty Address." Lecture, Global Leadership Summit, Willow Creek, South Barrington, IL, August 14, 2013.

Lewis, C. S. *Mere Christianity*. New York: MacMillan, 1960.

Louw, Johannes P., and Eugene Albert Nida. *Greek-English Lexicon of the New Testament: Based on Semantic Domains.* New York, NY: United Bible Soc., 1989.

Mahaney, C. J. *Humility: True Greatness.* Sisters, OR: Multnomah Publishers, 2005. Kindle.

Maxwell, Sam. "The Glory Mirror" as taught on October 7th, 2014, Destiny Outreach Center, North Tazewell, VA.

Merriam-Webster. *Merriam-Webster's Collegiate Dictionary & Thesaurus.* Springfield, MA: Merriam Webster, 2003.

Meyer, F. B. *Christ in Isaiah.* Grand Rapids, MI: Zondervan, 1950.

Munroe, Myles. *The Glory of Living: Keys to Releasing Your Personal Glory.* Shippensburg, PA: Destiny Image Publishers, 2005.

Munroe, Myles. *The Pursuit of Purpose: Conflict and Consensus.* Shippensburg, PA.: Destiny Image Publishers, 2000. Kindle.

Murray, Andrew. *Humility.* Seattle, WA: CreateSpace, 2012. Kindle.

Nixon, R. E. "Glory." In *New Bible Dictionary*, by Derek R. W. Wood. 3rd ed. Downers Grove, IL: InterVarsity Press, 1996.

Papa, Matt. *Look and Live: Behold the Soul-Thrilling, Sin-Destroying Glory of Christ.* Grand Rapids: Baker Publishing Group, 2014.

Piper, John, and Jonathan Edwards. *God's Passion for His Glory: Living the Vision of Jonathan Edwards, with the Complete Text of The End for Which God Created the World.* Wheaton, IL: Crossway Books, 2006. Kindle.

Piper, John. Doctrine Matters: *Ten Theological Trademarks from a Lifetime of Preaching.* Minneapolis, MN: Desiring God, 2013. Kindle.

Ritzema, Elliot. *300 Quotations for Preachers.* Bellingham, WA: Lexam Publishers, 2013. Electronic.

Ross, Tim. "Ambition vs Burden." YouTube. 2015. Accessed February 23, 2016. https://www.youtube.com/watch?v=EXrfKWFt-Ys.

Sheets, Dutch. *The Pleasure of His Company: A Journey to Intimate Friendship with God.* Grand Rapids, MI: Bethany House, 2014. Kindle.

Spicq, Ceslas, and James D. Ernest. *Theological Lexicon of the New Testament.* Peabody, MA: Hendrickson, 1994.

Spurgeon, Charles Haddon. *Gleanings Among the Sheaves.* New York, NY: Sheldon and Company, 1869.

Stott, John R. W. *The Cross of Christ*. Downers Grove, IL: InterVarsity Press, 1986.

Strong, James. *The Enhanced Strong's Lexicon*. Bellingham, WA: Logos Research Systems, 2015. Electronic.

Tzu, Sun. *The Art of War: Classic Collector's Edition*. Translated by Lionel B. Giles. El Paso, TX: El Paso Norte Press, 2009.

Vine, W. E., Merrill F. Unger, and William White. *Vine's Complete Dxpository Dictionary of Old and New Testament Words: With Topical Index*. Nashville: Thomas Nelson, 1996.